The Teacher's Lounge

The *Real* Role of Educators in Your Schools

Dr. John B. Gordon III

Clovercroft Publishing

Acknowledgments

This book is dedicated to my parents,
Mr. John B. Gordon Jr. and Mrs. Marian J. Bey Gordon
for instilling in me the importance of education
in my life. The Teacher's Lounge could not have
been completed without the loving support from
my wife Shavonne and my kids-Marcus, Kennedy,
and Simone who provide me the inspiration that
I need to be the best educator that I can be.

The Teacher's Lounge: The Real Roles of Educators in Your Schools

©2018 by Dr. John B. Gordon III

Published by Clovercroft Publishing, Franklin, Tennessee

Edited by Adept Content Solutions

Cover Illustration by Kennedy M. Gordon

Cover and Interior Design by Adept Content Solutions

Printed in the United States of America

ISBN: 978-1-948484-46-6

Contents

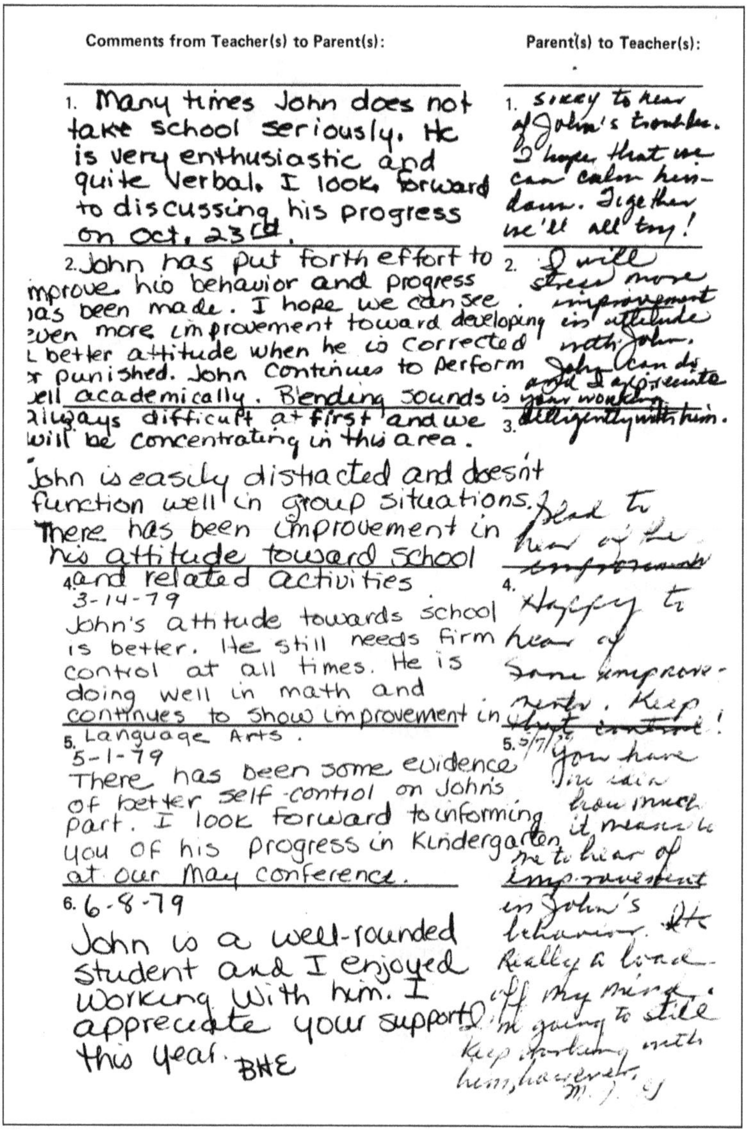

Comments from Teacher(s) to Parent(s):	Parent(s) to Teacher(s):
1. Many times John does not take school seriously. He is very enthusiastic and quite verbal. I look forward to discussing his progress on Oct. 23rd.	1. Sorry to hear of John's troubles. I hope that we can calm him down. Together we'll all try!
2. John has put forth effort to improve his behavior and progress has been made. I hope we can see even more improvement toward developing a better attitude when he is corrected or punished. John continues to perform well academically. Blending sounds is always difficult at first and we will be concentrating in this area.	2. I will stress more improvement in attitude with John. John can do and I appreciate your working diligently with him.
3. John is easily distracted and doesn't function well in group situations. There has been improvement in his attitude toward school and related activities	3. Glad to hear of the improvement
4. 3-14-79 John's attitude towards school is better. He still needs firm control at all times. He is doing well in math and continues to show improvement in Language Arts.	4. Happy to hear of some improvements. Keep that control!
5. 5-1-79 There has been some evidence of better self-control on John's part. I look forward to informing you of his progress in Kindergarten at our May conference.	5. 5/7/79 You have no idea how much it means to me to hear of improvement in John's behavior. It's really a load off my mind. I'm going to still keep working with him, however. M. J. [illegible]
6. 6-8-79 John is a well-rounded student and I enjoyed working with him. I appreciate your support this year. BHE	

Starting school at Maude Trevett was a little different than being the preacher's grandson in nursery school. Take a look at the dialogue between Mrs. Edwards and my mom. They worked together to get me more acclimated to the school routine.

Intro

This is not your ordinary book that discusses the trials and tribulations of educational leaders or data-driven statistics about the status of our youth. It will offer an in-depth perspective on the issues currently facing the field of education with a personal and humorous twist. In education, it has probably been said thousands of times that if we do not laugh, we will cry. There are so many sad school-related stories out there that do not have the happy endings that we remember from the feel-good decade of the 1980s. Think about all those movies such as the *Breakfast Club*, *Weird Science*, and *Back to the Future* (and all the sequels) that had our heroes and heroines experience great despair, heartbreak, or just plain old bad luck. Of course, due to the grit, resilience, and more than likely some assistance from a weird-looking sidekick who helped the lead character's triumph in the end, these movies always had a happy ending. Today, we deal with children of the 1990s, early 2000s, and 2010s, who were born in a decade of in-your-face TV and media that did not pull any punches or leave any stone unturned. The culture of the 1990s was based on challenging the political views, fighting Reaganomics, and learning how to survive as the new millennium was approaching. The culture of the 2000s and 2010s was based on exploring technology, making improvements on old ideas, and finding the easiest solutions to the toughest problems. We began to explore more risks in the 2000s after we realized that we had the technological capacity to do anything.

The fear of Y2K was greater than that of taking the geometry test that you forgot to study for all weekend, or the fear of getting cut from the basketball team when you knew you were better than everyone else, but still believed that you would get cut because the coach did not like you. The parents of the 1990s wanted to make sure that their children had it all. They would not allow some of the stereotypes that haunted them throughout their own educational careers to affect their children. They would protect them at all costs! This gave birth to the helicopter parent. Yes, those parents who seemed to have perfect attendance at their children's school. These were the parents who teachers knew on a first name basis, and caused administrators to cringe when their number popped up on an invention called caller ID. These parents always were active members of the PTSA and seemed to volunteer for events and activities even when the volunteer list was already full. The helicopter parent looked for the loophole. They did not want their children to fail, and if possible, they would do all of this without their children having knowledge. Did this make life easier for the student? Did the student ever have the opportunity to learn things on their own, or experience failure to build stronger character? To a helicopter parent, "character" was something that only occurred in drama class. My child will be the best they can be. They will be at the top of their class, president of this club, and captain of this team. It is my job to see what I can do to ensure that this happens. So, I will hover. Yes, hover around his/her friends, hover around the school, and of course, I will hover around the mall when my child is hanging out. My child will not even notice, because I am wearing tennis shoes, and using the mall as my personal track. I will blend in. They won't even know I am here. Were you, or are you one of these helicopter parents and you did not even know it?

Most teachers really do have a desire to educate our youth. Some have a desire to obtain a job that allows them to still get paid when they are not actually working during the summer months. My mother used to say that being in education was the only job she knew of that meant you did not have to go to work when the weather was bad, you always had your weekends and holidays off, and you got the chance to work with kids who would keep you looking young. She was right. The day I stopped teaching and went into administration was the day I got my first gray hair. Hopefully, as you read this book, you will be able to remember that one teacher in your life who really made a difference for you. You know, the teacher who had that lasting impression. I was lucky; I had two. For me, it was Mrs. Giannini, my twelfth grade Government teacher. She made me want to be a history teacher. The way she used current events and her sense of humor made me want to come back and visit her after I went to college. I think my favorite part of her class was Mock Congress, where we took on the role of a senator from an assigned state. I had Florida, and I can still remember all the details of us sitting in the auditorium to this day. It was so much fun, as we had another class in Mock Congress with us. I loved how Mrs. Giannini participated with us and was a senator from whatever state was left over after all of us chose. We tried so many times to stump her in class to see if she really did know what was going on in her state. If you were successful, you received bonus points, which almost guaranteed you an A. So much fun. Every time I see her, I make sure I thank her for allowing me to be myself in class and teaching me to appreciate the United States government. What she didn't know was that I also appreciated her role as a teacher.

The same can be said about Mr. Tim Donahue, my high school Psychology and Advanced Psychology teacher. He served as wrestling coach and was very well respected by the faculty. I point this out because he was only like 5'3", but he had great classroom management skills and told great stories that related to psychology in class. I remember watching movies like *Sybil* and *One Flew over the Cuckoo's Nest* like it was yesterday. I loved impersonating him in class because he had this nasally tone when he talked. It was even funnier because he was a pretty tough but short guy, so the entire class said that he sounded like a kid with a cold. The instructional strategies that he used in class made me fall in love with psychology. I majored in it once I arrived at the University of Virginia, and it was one of the best decisions that I ever made.

My perspective on education is slightly skewed because both of my parents were educators. My father taught math classes at Virginia Union University after he retired from being a District Supervisor for C&P Telephone (now Verizon). My mother also taught math at the high school level, became a math specialist, and eventually became a principal of an elementary school in the city of Richmond, Virginia. They made it very clear to me and my sisters that education is the key to success. Without education, more doors will close, people will look at you differently, and you will not be respected. These messages rang true in the Gordon household, where obtaining good grades was mandatory. If you had poor grades, you could not go outside and play with your friends. You could not watch TV, or worse, you could not play Nintendo. *Gasp!* The horror and shrewdness of this type of punishment! It kept my sisters and I extremely motivated, so much that both of my sisters finished in the top ten of their class during their high school careers and went to the colleges of their choice. That is key: the college of their choice, instead of having only one college to attend, or no college at all.

My grades were not as strong during my high school career as compared to my two sisters. I knew what I had to do, and sometimes just enough to get by, but I did not really begin to go that extra mile academically until my junior year. When I saw what the average GPA was to get into UVA or Virginia Tech, I knew I had to step it up. My work was cut out for me, as I had a little over a 2.0 GPA at the time. My mom and father told me that just in case the basketball scholarship did not work out, I would need to have something to fall back on. As usual, my parents were right. They weren't helicopter parents, because they let me fail to teach me a lesson, but they had very high standards for their children. Their formula worked, because all three of their children are now doctors.

My oldest sister, Rhea Gordon Miles, is a professor of Chemistry at East Carolina University. She always had the gift of gab, lived to be in the spotlight, and was very stubborn. Once she set her mind to something, you better believe it was going to happen. She was also very creative, and did great presentations for her projects, especially when she won the state 4-H competition with her Carol Burnett cooking in the kitchen routine.

My middle sister Donna Gordon Newsome is a neurologist in the Dallas/Fort Worth area. She always was the smartest of all three of us. During her senior year at Hermitage High School, she was ranked first in her class for most of the year. To my knowledge, she had a chance to be the first African-American valedictorian in Hermitage High School history. I did not know this was such a big deal, since I was a middle schooler at Brookland Middle School, and all I was concerned about was dealing with acne (that came out of nowhere) and making the basketball team. I realized this "first in the class" story was huge when other people started to talk about what it would mean to have "a black" as the valedictorian, and how some others were very upset about this possibility. So much, that research was conducted (at the suggestion of a rival student's family) into her full academic transcript dating back to eighth grade. Come to find out, a class that Donna took in eighth grade did not carry as much academic weight as the class that the rival student (from another locality) took when he was in eighth grade. She finished third in her class that year, but still attended the University of Virginia and majored in chemical engineering. She decided to go into medicine, specifically with a focus on the brain due to our grandparents suffering strokes and other brain diseases. Her educational motivation came from her sense of family and wanting to find a cure for the brain issues that took our grandparents from us. The day she got her medical degree from the Medical College of Virginia was one of the proudest days of my father's life. I know because he told me.

The risks that we had to endure in the 1980s and 1990s were minor in comparison to the risks my parents had to take during the civil rights movement. My father graduated at the top of his class, so he was able to give Donna advice when she was going through the first in the class investigation. We were very irritated, but not surprised, that the investigation occurred. It goes to show there were still challenges that minority students faced in the suburbs that had not changed for decades. I guess when you think about it, there were not a lot of differences between what a lot of students had to face in the city of Richmond versus what some had to face in the county of Henrico. My mother spoke about the risks of teaching in Richmond Public Schools after she had been a stay-at-home mom for several years after I was born. Going into the inner city to teach is tough enough for anyone, but even tougher for someone who had been out of it for a while to raise her kids. As soon as I was old enough to start school, she decided it was time to go back to work.

My mom told me that she wanted to go back to teaching because she missed it. She was a good teacher, but I think she also realized that it cost a lot of money to raise three kids in the '70s, '80s, and '90s. I am not sure if my father was making enough money to truly give us what we wanted, but I know we had enough to take care of what we needed. My father was the third African-American to graduate from the University of Virginia graduate programs.

He took the risk to attend a university where he would be judged by the color of his skin more than by the functions of his brain. He did it to make his life better, and ultimately to make our lives better. He took an educational risk in the 1960s that would affect the educational opportunities that his children could have in the 1980s and, of course, today.

So today, is the focus more on accountability or on truly educating our students? It's almost as if the research is split down the middle. I am sure we can find articles and studies that can prove that instructional accountability has had a direct correlation on student achievement. However, I am positive that we can find research that supports a loss of student engagement, creativity, and overall enthusiasm for learning because of high accountability standards. In the end, both sides create anxiety and risks for the overall plight of education. Who is more at risk? The poor minority student who has a father in jail and a mom who is working two jobs while she is pregnant with her fourth child, or the rich student whose father is a CEO of a major company, travels a lot, and leaves all the child-rearing to the stay-at-home mom who does not feel the love from her husband but finds medication from the downstairs bar? Or the kid who does enough to get by, does not want to stick out in the crowd, does not want to draw any attention to themselves, and is happy with being "average"? Are all these students at risk? Is one more at risk than the others?

Are teachers and administrators now at risk because of the increasing levels of accountability? What happens to a new teacher who is teaching their first "state test" and does not meet the cut-score for pass rates? Will this teacher be placed on an improvement plan? Will they be shunned by the other teachers because they had low scores? Will they be fired? Or will they just say that teaching is not for them and decide not to return? What happens to the administrator who has had struggling scores in their building the last two years, mainly due to a high turnover in teachers, or a cohort of students who have not performed well academically since the third grade? Is the principal going to be moved? Will the state take over? All these issues are very prevalent in education today. It is more than students at risk—it is now education at risk. It is our job to take a hard look at the roles of everyone who is involved in a child's education.

Due to the sensitive nature of some of the topics that will be discussed in what will soon become one of your favorite books, some of the names and identities have been changed to protect the innocent (and the not so innocent). I am sure you will enjoy a nice mix of educational history, tips for instructional success, and insight into the future of education. Hopefully your brainstorms will lead to suggestions that eliminate the internal risks of our current education models. As you progress through this book, be prepared to take planned breaks to engage in reflection questions, scenarios, or other activities that relate to the chapter and your own personal experiences. In the Intro, you read about the major educational experiences that occurred in my family that motivated me to go into education. Please take the time to reflect upon the following:

Intro Reflections

1) Who were the most influential people in your educational career growing up? Did these people lead you to focus on the career that you have today?

2) Think about a few of the major events that happened in your childhood. How did you handle them? Did you become more motivated or did you avoid these issues to better cope with the situation?

3) What was the main reason that you purchased this book? Are you more curious about the current state of education or about the current mindset of today's youth?

Chapter 1

Students of Today

There's a saying that "kids will always be kids." This rings true in many circumstances, but today's student has many more issues to deal with than the students of the 1960s, 1970s, or 1980s. The students of the 1990s, 2000s, and 2010s have all had to deal with anything or everything happening on a larger scale. The culprit is technology. Back in the day, if something embarrassing happened, like tripping and falling in front of your classmates or peers at school, of course everyone would laugh, and some would probably talk about it for a couple of days. The victim in this case would of course be mortified for being embarrassed in front of a large group of people, but things would usually be over in a short time, and everyone would forget about it. Not today. You know someone filmed it! Due to the invention of cell phones, flip-cams, and of course the internet, the victim's peers can review this random act of clumsiness over and over. Students are so creative, and sometimes can be cruel, and will probably add humorous captions to the fall such as "Timber!" or "Drop it like it's hot," or something like that. Some future filmmakers may have zoomed in on the victim's face just to show the pure agony or slowed the entire act down for a more gradual comedic effect. And because it was filmed, of course it was posted on the internet. The students of today live for social media. Social media magnifies the everyday happenings of student life a hundred-fold as compared to the generation that grew up in the 1960s–1990s.

I honestly believe that many times the students of today do not realize that what they are posting can be harmful, that some may view it as bullying, or that what they say can be used against them in a court of law. To them, it is just fun. "Hey, check this out" is the main theme. Usually it is done to get a reaction from the internet public, and they are hoping to get a like or a retweet, or to be favorited. These are the things that the students of today strive for.

It is still true that students want to do well in school. All students still want to have good grades, but now there are so many more distractions that prevent this from becoming a reality. It can still be argued that there are several benefits of growing up in today's educational society. Students of today can complete research in a shorter period. The days of finding the best encyclopedia for your information are long gone. If a class that you want to take does not fit in your grueling schedule, no problem; it is almost guaranteed to be offered online through a variety of online institutions. Of course, there might be a little fee that is associated with taking these courses. This option then becomes a socio-economic issue.

The students of today also do not see color—at least, not most of the time. It is not a big deal when two students from two different races develop a romantic interest in each other. In my experience the only issues that develop come from their parents, or older relatives that do not think this is a "good idea." What the parents or older relatives fail to realize is that this is not the 1970s or 1980s or even the 1990s. The millennials, as they are commonly known, only see someone who they are attracted to. The terminology for this generation of students continues to change. As recently as 2012, I began to hear our current group of kids being referred to as Generation Z. I think my parents' generation were known as the baby boomers, and I think those of us in our forties are referred to as Generation X. So, what happened to Generation Y?

The students of today do not identify with the racial challenges of the prior generations because they are more focused on the public challenge of not having their business posted on the web. Society of Generation Z includes the online society that tends to have more access to our students than they probably should. For some of our kids, the challenge of staying connected to the "real world" or documenting every major, and sometimes minor event in their lives as if they need a timestamp. As you can see, challenges still exist for students. It's just a different type of challenge now. However, I must admit that since we have a had a change in government, many of the racial stereotypes and even some of the vulgar language has returned to the forefront. It is almost as if some students feel empowered to use racial epithets or are threatened that the United States of America is becoming too much of a melting pot. When these issues arose in the classroom or on the sports fields, we used to say that those things must be learned at home. However, with the ability to research any nationalist group, or organizations dedicated to the concept of racial superiority, the students could be getting this information from anywhere. It is our job as parents and as educators, to teach acceptance and not tolerance. To see people and not color. Or as my grandmother used to say, see someone for what they are on the inside, and not what is on the outside. This always rang very true for me as several people I have met throughout my life were kind of surprised to see that I was an African-American when they met me. I guess the name of John B. Gordon III can cover many ethnicities. Maybe it is when they see that I am a proud member of Kappa Alpha Psi, Inc. that they get a little insight into the fact that maybe he is black.

As many of the students do not see color, they also do not see sexuality. It used to be such a taboo if students thought that other students were "gay." In some cases, it became a covert operation for someone to see if they can prove if the person was gay or not. Now because of the openness of sexuality, it is not uncommon to see same sex couples holding hands in school, or kissing, or attending dances together. There is a fine line however as today's students tend to be more accepting of lesbians than they are of gay men. It could be because adolescent men are still developing their own identities and must wear the "mask" more to fit in. If you check out the status of many students aged 15-22 on the web, some may describe their sexual status as "fluid" or "androgynous." Should young teens, and teenagers really be discussing that on social media?

At the high school level, some female students will report that a large percentage of their girls' basketball teams or softball teams are lesbians. It doesn't stop them from trying out or wanting to play the sport, it is just something that is accepted with this group of girls. However, their parents may see things a little different. During my twenty-two years as an educator, I have had dozens of parents meet or communicate with me that they are concerned that if their daughter joins this team or that team, that they are going to try and "turn my child gay." I am not sure if it is my place to explain that being gay is not a choice, but an internal feeling or knowledge that the individual has. It is not like religion, where you can be converted. The gay students and family members that I have spoken with have all said that they just knew from day one. I guess certain things excited them sexually and it just so happened to be a same-sex thought or experience. Many times, those thoughts were about one of their close friends who just so happens to be heterosexual. The sad part is that the students many times do not see homosexuality as big of a deal as their parents did. It is almost as if the students had to deal with the stereotypes or fear from their parents more than the actual pressure of being in the locker room with someone who might be attracted to them. This was brought to a head when the government in North Carolina determined that transgender students had to use the bathroom of the gender in which they were born. Several parents met with me during my time as a principal and inquired if we had any transgender students at the school, because they wanted to make sure their child was not exposed to that "stuff." In the most professional way that I could respond, I politely explained that I could not share that information because it was not something that we tracked. I also had to remind the parents that we treated all children the same regardless of sexual orientation, that it is the parent's job to protect their children, but today's students want to learn from discovery, their own life experiences, and they want to be able to make their own decisions. I know that this does not sound like anything new from any generation of kid, but in my experience a lot of the students do a pretty good job of explaining their goals, their plan to achieve them, and their naivety in the cost or resources that will be necessary. This is where parents gain their child's trust by explaining the costs of their current lifestyle and by showing them how much those luxury items that they see on TV actually cost. Lastly, parents can share the average starting salaries for the field that their children eventually would like to do, or even the difference in earning potential for a high school graduate vs. a college graduate.

The students of today want good jobs that will allow them to make good money, and maybe meet a celebrity or two. Some would argue that the students of today want the good jobs, but do not want the hard work that comes along with getting a good job. I have heard many students say that ideally, they would like to make $100k a year, working from home. Maybe they have seen too many of those infomercials or other advertisements that offer this great opportunity to the masses. Other students are also hoping that they can get these good jobs with only having a high school diploma, or at most a bachelor's degree. These are not the same students who have a plan for going directly into the workforce, only after they obtain this special certification. They understand that you need some type of training to get the good jobs. Only those that want to be doctors and lawyers have mentioned that they are willing to go to grad school to obtain their goals. Most of today's students believe that grad school is nothing more than an opportunity to create more debt for themselves. It is too early to document in this great book that you are reading, that today's students feel an overwhelming sense of entitlement as it relates to what their parents will pay for, and what they are willing to pay for. President Obama won such a high percentage of the "young vote" due to the economic plan that he put in place for those voters ages 18-25. Providing recent college graduates, or those who are just entering the work force, the option to stay on their parent's insurance until age 25 was key. I do not believe that today's students really understand just how much benefits cost, or the fact that they do not have those insurance costs coming out of their bi-weekly checks. Every little bit helps, especially when they get the letter from the federal government alerting them that their first payment on the student loan they thought was free money is due soon.

So, what role does the teacher play in developing the students of today? Besides being the role models, or the hardest teacher you will ever have, teachers must find a way to build relationships with students, without crossing over into the realm of being perceived as a friend. Depending on the level of teacher, specifically elementary or secondary, the teacher must be a constant in the student's life. It has been determined with numerous studies how the school is a foundation for children ages ten to eighteen. The different roles that the teacher eventually takes on will vary from day to day. In speaking with hundreds of my colleagues over the years, the teacher will describe the days when they serve as the mother: "Did you brush your teeth this morning?"

That question usually follows the "Good morning" conversation that all teachers are asked to have with their students as they enter the room in the morning.

Teachers at the elementary level are a little franker with this question than teachers at the secondary level. Elementary teachers will be direct and ask little Johnny if he brushed his teeth or washed his face because they can still see the drool marks or crust on the side of the child's mouth. Then of course the discussion then evolves into what type of parent would allow their child to leave the house like that. Secondary school teachers will take their hands and cover their noses when the student says" Hi Mr. Gordon" as the wind from the "H" sound hits their noses and the teacher smells air that resembles manure. I always would ask the kid, "What did you eat for breakfast?" with such edginess that other kids in the class would sometimes snicker. I would then usually follow up with a reach into my desk drawer while handing the kid a mint as I took roll. At the secondary level, we must be subtle so that the kid does not lash out.

Students want to be taught. Students want to be taught well. But if they know the teacher is weak, they will go for blood like sharks in water. The first couple of weeks of school are always very important in setting the tone in the classroom. Students also use this time to get a feel for the teacher, determine if the class is hard, and figure out where they fit in the class both socially and academically. Students know that at some point and time they will have to participate in collaborative groups, so they begin to develop strategies to ensure that they will not be in a group with a bunch of idiots, or the kid who smells bad, or the kid who Mr.

Gordon keeps handing mints because he has bad breath. They will usually try to establish their seating arrangements based on the proximity to their friends, their proximity to the front or back of the room (depending on if they have preferential seating because of their IEP or 504 plan), or their proximity to the door so that they can see if any of their "real" friends will be passing by soon and they can communicate with them while they are in the hall. All of this happens in the first couple of days of school where students literally stake out their territory. It is almost as if there is a certain level of "student politics" that exists now that is more than the level of cliques that we have all witnessed on television. The groups of students are more than the jocks, the nerds, the future leaders of America, etc. Now it is more like a cross section of all of those with additional traits that do not fit the norm. The captain of the football team is now the president of the Science club. Students sit with other students who are like them in the cafeteria. Students feel very comfortable having candid conversations with their teachers about topics that some would consider very personal. They talk to their teachers about issues like this because they don't want their friends to judge them, or they believe their friends may be too immature to handle the issue confidentially. I can think of dozens of incidents in which teachers were the first to know that a student was pregnant, or that a relative of one of their students was going to jail or had terminal cancer. If the student knows that the teacher cares, then they will share.

Students want to be taught individually. The old-fashioned model of having a one-size-fits-all mentality, or having the teacher stand up and talk for forty-five or ninety minutes, has been proven to not be conducive to all students. Students of today want to be given direction, want to be helped when they get stuck or do not understand something, and then want to be left alone to figure things out or fill in the gaps. They do not want teachers hovering over them. They want to feel a sense of independence, even if it is a little false. Those teachers who assign projects and provide a rubric of what must be included within the project or assignment practice this belief. The teacher should serve as the facilitator of information, or more as a guide, and then let the students discover things as they work. Now due to the high levels of accountability, the teacher must make sure they cover everything that is written in the Holy Trinity of education: state standards, curriculum maps, and pacing guides. However, the teacher must take into consideration the learning style of the student, the creativity of the student, and the amount of instructional time that will be allotted before the teacher must move the class on to the next topic or unit.

If the student of today is learning, then they will be able to teach the student of tomorrow. Whether it is their children, or if they desire to go into the field of education, if they know the content they should be able to teach. I know for a fact that many of my teachers were completely shocked when they found out that I went into education. I honestly believe that they knew I was smart enough, it's just that they could not picture it. For some, they still saw me as the student in their class that would try to crack a joke at a moment's notice, and then blame the students around me for laughing and drawing attention to us. Of course, when the report card would come out six weeks later, and I had the "x" under works without disturbing others, I would quickly tell my parents "they put that down because I laugh at Titus' jokes." I had to find some way to make sure that I wasn't going to be put on punishment for acting up in school. Regardless if my grades were good (and they usually were) if I had behavioral issues that was the same as getting a "D" in my parent's eyes. It was my responsibility to make sure that I went to school every day, kept up with my work-especially during basketball and track season, and did not act a fool in class. If I did not perform well in all three areas, then things were not good for me. My parents made me understand that even if we are smart, we will not succeed if we can't be counted on or taken seriously. This is where the perfect attendance (for eleven years, I might add) came in. My father knew I had a strong sense of humor, but he always wanted to remind me that there was a time and place to be funny, and the classroom was not one of them. He would usually give me speeches like this after he had worked an eleven-hour day at C&P Telephone while he was getting undressed. For some reason, these father/son talks carried more meaning because he would always take his belt off first and sit it beside me on the couch. A subtle reminder. One that I think I used with my son several times when his grades began to slip in high school. OMG! I became my dad.

Reflection Questions

"Students of Today"

1) Take some time to think how you would describe the students of today. Do you see any similarities? What do you think is their biggest challenge?

2) As a parent, mentor, role model, or just as an average adult that loves kids, what do you think is the hardest part about building relationships with kids?

3) What advice would you give a student who is very active on social media? (In your answer, you must be more creative than saying don't get an account.)

4) How do you think *your* parents would have answered question number one? Are there any similarities between your response and their response?

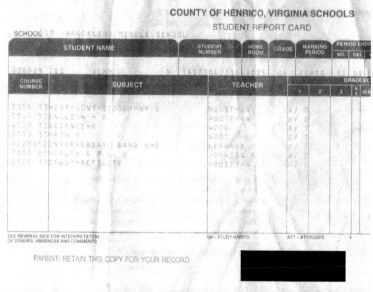

This is when I began to come into my own. I had some say in what I wore in the picture, I thought the pink shirt with the yellow tie was kind of *Miami Vice* Like. Oh, check the report card, Honor Roll was in full effect!

Chapter 2

The Parents

Parents are supposed to be the adults. They are supposed to guide their children and help them make the right decisions in their lives. Parents used to be at least twenty plus years older than their children. Supposedly, parents are to be calm, and understand the different issues that their children face. In the 1960s and 1970s, parents would see the teachers, administrators, and other people who worked at the school at church, the grocery store, or out on an afternoon run. Back then was the time of the true school community when everyone worked together for the betterment of the child. The plan was for the children to want to come back to the community and raise children of their own. A never-ending cycle of support and generations of knowledge was supposed to be passed down through the years. The children would tell stories to their children of how their parents raised them in this community and how the school was like an extension of the home. Parents were huge supporters of the schools, the administration, and the teacher. This was the peak period of parents being the first teachers and understanding the partnerships, family atmosphere, and community trust needed for schools and students to be successful. But in the 1990s, it all changed. Some historians might say that this change was due to the increase in single parent homes, more teenage pregnancies, and a change in home values. Parents of the 1990s were coming in to schools dressed like they just came from the club. And the funny part is, the parent was asked to come in due to repeat dress code violations for the daughter. Now we see where the daughter gets it from. If a teacher called home before 1990, the discussion with the teacher was the eleventh commandment, and the child would be sure to pay, and the behavior would be corrected. The child probably would have to write a note apologizing to the teacher and offer to volunteer at the school for some community service. After 1990, the parent would take the side of the child, say that the teacher was picking on their child, and in many cases, curse the teacher out or hang up on them. The parent would become very possessive on who or how their child could be disciplined. They wanted to protect their children from any negative things that they thought could affect their lives, even if the negative things were based on something that the child needed to correct. It was like the parents did not want their children to have growing pains, but instead be perfect in every way. In looking back, maybe the parent was trying to protect their child from failure.

In my experience, failure is often the best teacher. I know that my failure of not making the middle school basketball team in sixth and seventh grade motivated me to work on my game even more. I can still vividly remember the night of cut-day in my sixth-grade year. Coach Madison called all the names of the players who should report to

As an 8th grader-left, you really do believe you are the big man on campus. Still hurt to not be on the basketball team though. 9th grade-right, looks a little different even though it is one year apart. I began to have a lot of confidence here. And look, for some reason I must have thought I was really cool as I had on a gold chain in 8th grade, and a silver one in 9th.

practice the next day, one by one. All of us that were left were told that we had huge flaws in our game and that we had a lot of work to do to make the team. When I looked around the gym, everyone that got cut was sort of expected to get cut because they couldn't play. But I could. Everyone at the time told me that there was no way that I should have been cut. I cried that night so hard. Both my mom and dad came in and told me that it was going to be OK, and that I could play for Virginia Randolph (little league) instead. I couldn't stop crying. I knew that it must have hurt them too, because everyone kept offering me ice cream to try to make me feel better. Man, I even turned that down. I must have really have been heartbroken if I turned down my favorite (Breyer's mint chocolate chip). It took a while to get over not making the team, but it also made me work harder so that when I got to high school, I was one of the best players on the team. If it wasn't for the failure that my parents allowed me to experience, I may not have been as motivated to continue to work on my game the way I did. I think my parents also realized that based on the amount of emotion that I displayed when I got cut, that I really loved the game of basketball. From that day forward, they also supported me more in my quest to become better.

Many parents of the 1990s would over-empathize with their children and compare it to something that happened to them when they were in school that they thought was unfair. Psychologically it was if they were getting pay-back for their own past indiscretions and taking it out on their child's teacher. What did the teacher do to deserve this negativity? Would some teachers take this verbal and emotional beating personally and decide that the parent just had a problem with them? How would the teacher handle this situation? The teacher would probably just write down several emotional comments on their parent contact log and move on to calling the next parent. Now the teacher would usually be thankful that they made these calls only from the school phone, because they did not want the parents nor their students to have their home or cell numbers. Maybe it wasn't until the teacher arrived to work the next day and during a routine discussion in the teacher's lounge, they discovered that many of their colleagues had felt the wrath of this parent before. It was almost as if having a normal, non-confrontational conversation with the parent would become the rarity.

When did making parents aware of the difficulties of their children become a crime? In my experiences, I have seen all sides of parental involvement from the parent who you know will be there on the first day of school through the 176th day, to the parent you only know by voice because you always get their voicemail, to the parent who only comes in when they can't do anything with the child at home, and want you to solve the problem. The spectrum and the different layers change all the time. Parental involvement is key in a student's education. The parent must understand the thin line that cannot be crossed regarding a student's independence, learning ability, and expectations. Therefore, constant communication between parent and student is so important. This communication must happen regardless of the age of the student. Parents must try to remain as proactive as possible, and not just react to the teacher phone call, or worse, the semi-annual parent-teacher conferences (cue iconic horror music here). I always appreciated the parents who brought their children with them to parent-teacher conferences at the high school level. They were the parents who would listen so attentively when the teacher would start relaying information that the student had been withholding, and of course the squirming of the kid would always be priceless. By nature, parents want to defend their children, but the parent who knows how the system works and waits until they have all the information before they make a judgement are the parents who make strong partners in education. In the previous example, when it was found that the child was wrong, this was always the perfect time for the parent and teacher to work together. However, this scenario only worked when the teacher had enough courage to tell Mr. and Mrs. Gordon that little Johnny didn't turn in his project because he was sent out of class for writing notes to his girlfriend. Some teachers get intimidated by parents so much that they are afraid to tell the truth. The teacher tries to shy away from any potential conflict, or avoid the situation all together, which makes things even more frustrating for the parent. The hesitation could be due to past siblings in which the parent and teacher disagreed over the older sibling's academic potential, or worse yet, behavior in the class. The parent might not be as bad as Beverley Goldberg from the ABC show *The Goldbergs,* but in their mind, they might as well be.

Don't be the parent who jumps to conclusions before they have all the information. Parents should provide support to their children, but they should also provide support to the teacher. The partnership that is supposed to exist between parent and teacher will need to be based on trust and constant levels of communication. When discussing things with the teacher, parents should remain professional or polite in the public setting and then become frank with their children or even the teacher behind closed doors. Teachers make mistakes too, but things do not have to be compounded by becoming argumentative, rude, or confrontational. All teachers and administrators want some level of parental involvement if the clearly defined roles and or limitations are explained. There are usually issues when parents try to tell teachers how to do their jobs, believe that everything about their class or teaching style is wrong or not the way that things should be done. Parents should remember how they would feel if the teacher came to their profession and confronted them about their job, even though the parent was the expert. The same level of respect should occur for teachers.

Parents should help their children develop a school routine at an early age. This includes setting the bedtime for school sometime during the summer, deciding who is going to make lunch and what ingredients will be included, when the child will take a shower (in the morning or at night). Most importantly, the parent must find a way to confirm that the shower actually occurred. My wife, Shavonne, and I had to find this out the hard way with my son Marcus. For some reason, he would claim that he was taking a shower every night, but his hair would still stink the next morning. At first, I thought that Marcus was just forgetting to wash his hair, but later I discovered that Marcus was not washing his entire body at all. So, one school evening, when he was

I still remember this day like it was yesterday. I had to grow up really fast since Marcus was born during my senior year of high school. I think this is when I realized that I wasn't just living for me anymore.

going to take his shower around 7:30 p.m. (we developed a routine), I went to the bathroom door and got on all fours. The shower water was running, and this dude even had the nerve to sing in the bathroom like he was in the shower. As I looked under the door, I could see Marcus' feet in his flip-flops tapping away to the song that he was singing. He turned off the water, after he made sure his washcloth was wet, he then got up from the toilet that he was sitting on and walked to the door to leave the bathroom. I couldn't get off my old basketball knees fast enough. He opened the door, and there I was. I quickly went into father mode and used my father's voice: "Boy, if you don't get back in there and actually wash your butt, I am going to kill you!" The look on his face was of pure astonishment and fear. Mission accomplished. We never had to worry about him faking a wash again. The new struggle was getting him to take a shower every day. Especially for a middle school boy about to be in high school. Middle school boys stink more than elementary boys. And of course, high school boys who are about to be grown men stink the worst.

The school routine should also include the time to wake up in the morning, and what time to begin completing homework or any other school related project in the afternoon. The parent can give their children some input into developing the routine but should already have some time slots in mind. Now my parents had the classic rule of no TV or video games until after you have finished your homework. It made sense to use the TV and playing *Legend of Zelda* or *Double Dribble* as a reward for getting everything done. I think my mom forgot that I just might be hungry when I got home, especially after I ate lunch at 11:15 a.m., had PE during sixth period, and then would get home around 4. Sometimes she would even ask me, "Why are you so hungry?" or better yet, give me the classic threat of, "If you eat now, you are not getting any dinner." Wow, what a choice to make. Eat at 4 by myself, which probably would not have been more than a sandwich anyway or wait and eat around 7 with the rest of the family and hope I wouldn't get the broiled chicken wing that was too close to the burner in the oven. Tough choice. So, we usually compromised with some type of healthy snack such as Wheat Thins, or more likely some type of weight watchers' food, since somebody in my family was always on a diet. After completing my homework, I would then venture to my room to talk on the phone (you know I was cool because I had my own line: 804-261-8044), play video games (sometimes I had the Nintendo on all night so that I would not lose my place on *Castlevania*, because this was before you could save your progress on games), watch music videos on BET or MTV, or go outside and hang with my boys. The part about going outside and hanging with my boys would sometimes be a crapshoot because they didn't always finish their homework quickly, and then I wouldn't have anyone to play with. That was part of the reason why I began to excel at basketball; many days, I would just go out and work on my game by myself.

    The difficult part about developing a routine is knowing when to veer from it a little because you had to spend that extra time studying. My mother would make sure that part of us completing our homework would include reviewing our notes every day. That would usually be about ten to fifteen minutes per subject, which equaled about an hour and a half. If we had a test, I wouldn't look at the other subjects and just study for that test only. Sometimes my mother would ask me after I was done if I had studied, and regardless of the answer, she would make me go back to my room and study some more. Parents must understand that in assisting their children in developing school routines also includes the parent being there for assistance if necessary. My mom would usually go in her room and lay down, potentially waiting for me to come in with questions, or she would be downstairs making dinner. I had a slight advantage because she was an educator and was very familiar with the material that I was studying. I had some difficulty in my math classes once I got to Geometry because it was just so new to me. My mom could help me figure things out, but the downside was that it would take her so long to do it. This was because she had to take the time to relearn what she learned in high school or college.

Sometimes my dad would come home early enough to help too if there was a problem I could not figure out in Geometry. They would go into their bedroom and work the problem out on like six pieces of paper, and would take like thirty minutes to come out and give me the answer. To this day, I still wonder if they were working on Geometry, or was it really Biology? Their answers would always be right, but the other issue was that they were using a process that we did not learn in class, and that I did not understand. I could not take this back to my math teacher at Hermitage, who always made sure that we had to show our work and try to walk her through this. And because it took them thirty minutes and six pieces of paper, this meant that one problem would take up my entire class period on test day.

What a dilemma! Still, my parents took the time to assist me with my schoolwork, which needs to be a part of the school routine for children.

Lastly, parents should make sure they check their children's book bags and or notebooks every now and then. At the elementary level, this could potentially happen daily, as you are trying to instill the importance of your child being organized as well as making sure that you do not miss any important papers, fliers, grades, etc. It was good to know that during their elementary years, every Thursday I knew a packet/folder was coming home for Kennedy and Simone that had their graded papers for the week, and any fliers that discuss upcoming school events and activities. At the secondary level, it became a little more difficult. Children begin to wise up and will try to hide the bad grades by leaving those papers at school, on the bus, or worse, throwing them away. Then of course, everyone, including your child, is so shocked when the report card comes home, and the grades are below par. The parent checking their children's school belongings lets the child know that they are involved, care, and want to help them succeed.

Of course, these days, many parents can check their child's grades online anyway, so we will just keep that our little secret. The creation of parent portal, or whatever your school division calls it, provides many parents with insight into what is going on in the classroom, as well as a "look-ahead" for important due dates and assignments that are coming up. It is good for parents to be able to discuss these assignments with their children beforehand. However, parents must be careful of not crossing the line and invading their children's privacy, but that is where keeping the relationship with your child is important. Checking the book bags/notebooks will also provide insight into if your child is using drugs, has joined a gang, or clues to other potential negative behavior. The students of today still draw and doodle/graffiti on their school supplies, so you can always say that you just so happened to see it one day.

Parents helping to assist students to develop school routines help their children with time management, being prompt, and meeting deadlines. These are the skills that they will need when they go off to college, or go into the military, or when they finally get a job and can move out of your house. That is still the goal, right? All parents want their children to be successful and want to guide them with good advice and life lessons along the way. Parents should not be hands off when it comes to education, but should find ways to foster their children's independence both at school and at home. The parent will know that their plan has been successful when they no longer must remind their children of their routines, and they do things on their own. My oldest daughter, Kennedy, reached this point during her fifth grade year. She is very structured and sets dates and times on when she is going to do almost everything. She is very mature and is a straight A student. I wanted to make sure that she kept her flexibility of being a middle-school kid, and did not become so structured that she became inflexible. When that happens, you no longer run your routine; instead, your routine runs you.

Chapter 2

Parental Scenarios

Scenario 1: You have noticed a change in your child. Even though his/her grades have not suffered, they do not seem to share as much information with you as they have in the past. At first you think it is just becoming a teenager, but then you realize it is something more. It seems that your child has a new set of friends and does not speak highly about school anymore. Because of these new thoughts, they have withdrawn from their after-school activities and clubs. How do you handle this situation? What steps would you take to communicate with your child to find out what has happened?

Scenario 2: Your child has made it very clear that they would like to be a professional athlete when they grow up. You have provided the stats and research that show that how rare it is to reach that goal, and that the careers of professional athletes are very short. You also know that in watching your child compete, they have average athletic ability, and does not really have the passion that shows that they love the sport. Your child is still adamant that this is what they want to do and have asked you for $1000 to send them to one of the best camps in the country. How do you handle this situation? What additional information can you share with your child that can help both of you understand if this camp is necessary? How do you think your child will respond?

Maude Trevvett Elementary School

This Certifies That

JOHN GORDON

is awarded this Certificate for

S.C.A. TREASURER

Given at Maude Trevvett School this _6th_ day of _June_, A. D., 19 _84_

Marianne Knight

Robert Dunn
PRINCIPAL

Sandra P. Smith
TEACHER
Nellie Short

School Leadership is very important in student development. I thought I was the man as SCA treasurer since I was in control of the money. Little did I know that all I really did was add and subtract things from this big green ledger!

Chapter 3

The Teacher

As I mentioned earlier in this very entertaining, but practical book that you are reading, I come from a family of educators, and have always been told that education will open-up more doors than sometimes opportunities will allow. I think the understanding and knowing how important education would be to my future was really drilled home by my fifth grade teacher Mrs. Smith. I was lucky during my time at Maude Trevett Elementary School to have the same teacher for both my kindergarten and first grade years in Mrs. Edwards, to ending with Mrs. Smith who taught both of my sisters and knew my family really well. Mrs. Smith stood almost six feet tall (maybe she was like 5'8 but to a fifth grader she was six feet), was very direct, kind of intimidating, but she was also very nice. If you did things right and pleased her, you got all types of special privileges like going to clap the erasers out back and running notes on the other bad kids to the office. Wow. We lived to leave the classroom back then. All the other fifth grader teachers like Mrs. Jessup and Mrs. Witt respected Mrs. Smith who was like the de facto leader of the school.

I can still remember Mrs. Smith so vividly, especially our annual trip to Washington DC.

For our Washington DC field trip, each parent chaperone had five or six students. I hoped that I was going to be put into a group with Jason Pryor, Titus Cutler, Lamont Davis, or Sean and Juan Wright. Dang. Struck out on all of them. I was with Hao Vong, who was cool, but I didn't know him that well at the time, but worse we had to be with Amy who had a medical issue. Now all we could think about as fifth graders was that we were not going to be able to go to all the places because Amy's medical equipment would get in the way. Remember this is 1983 and the medical tripod filled with medicine that Amy was pushing around would be on her hip today. Amy did a good job of keeping up and moving around, so things did not turn out so bad. Until Amy's mom decided that she was hungry due to all the walking, she wanted to get a Shasta. I quickly let her know that Mrs. Smith said we were not to buy anything from the street vendors. I can remember Mrs. Smith scaring the hell out of all the kids in class one day by telling us the story of one of her students from many years ago that ate something from a street vendor, got robbed, and threw up on the bus all the way back to Maude Trevett because of food poisoning. Even though our parents gave us money, all of us swore that we would buy souvenirs from the museums only. As Amy's mom is sitting on the bench enjoying her Shasta and chips, Amy is eating popcorn, and everyone else in the group bought something too. Even Hao had a bag of chips because Amy's mom said it was ok. This turned into a master spy plan or something because Amy's mom rehearsed with Amy exactly what to say if we ran into Mrs.

Smith or any of the other teachers. She said, "Amy, we will tell them that you weren't feeling well and that your blood sugar was low. When I look at you, you say, 'I am feeling better now, mom.' They rehearsed it and everything.

When it was my turn to buy something, I refused. I was too scared to even think about it. It was as if I could hear Mrs. Smith looking over my shoulder and saying, "John Gordon. You better not." Amy's mom told me to get something to drink at least because it was so hot outside. I thought about it because it was hot, but I decided against it.

Literally five minutes later, as some of our group is throwing their trash away, who comes around the corner? Mrs. Smith! I think I got so scared that every drop of melanin left my body. Mrs. Smith walks so fast past me and she approached Amy's mom. Amy sees Mrs. Smith before her mom does and went right into her lead role: "I am feeling better now mommy," she says. Her mom just laughs because she had not seen Mrs. Smith yet and says, "Good job, Amy," as she laughs. "We don't have to practice anymore." As soon as the word "anymore" comes out of her mouth, she sees Mrs. Smith. Mrs. Smith pointed to the kids who were still eating and fussed at Amy's mom like she was one of her students in class. Amy's mom kind of felt like it too because she could not get a word in and all we could hear her say was "yes ma'am" several times. Mrs. Smith then points in the general direction towards the bus and makes sure all of us get on it. Our field trip got cut short because we didn't follow the directions. I couldn't believe it. There was still the air and space museum left on the tour. I was kind of mad, but I was more concerned if Mrs. Smith was going to tell my mom what happened. On the bus ride home, Mrs. Smith calls me to the back of the bus. I am thinking that she is now going to let me know that she was going to call my mom or worse, come to the car in person and tell her when my mom came to pick me up. Instead, Mrs. Smith told me she was proud of me. She said that Amy's mom told her that I was the only person not to get anything from the vendor. She apologized for me having to be punished for the poor decision of an adult, and that she was glad that I didn't follow the group. She even told me that I would get a plus on my behavior card for making good decisions. At the end of the year when she signed my yearbook she talked about how she was going to miss having the Gordon family at Trevett and that she knew we were destined for great things.

Coming from a family of educators can be both good and bad. My mother is a former Mathematics teacher, and my father also taught Math at the collegiate level. My mother used her passion for Mathematics to climb the education ladder to K-12 Math Specialist for Richmond City Public Schools, and then later to an assistant principal at the elementary level, and finally becoming the Principal of Elizabeth Redd Elementary School. Having both parents as educators, specializing in math, meant that I should have always done well in math. No excuses. Even when I had the worst Algebra II teacher in American history.

During my tenth grade year at Hermitage High School, I had Mrs. O'Bannon. She was what can be described as a veteran teacher who knew her subject area but had some classroom management issues when it came to "dealing" with students who were not considered "honors." At Hermitage High School in the late 1980s and early 1990s, the

I think this was the peak of my "chain game." This was during the time that if you have a Mercedes-Benz symbol as jewelry, you were the man!

honors classes were usually very homogenous, predominantly white students, with a few Asian and Black students sprinkled throughout a few periods. Now I was starting to hit a wall in my math classes as I was coming off a D in Geometry, even though I had one of the most dedicated teachers that a student could have in Mr. Howe. Mr. Howe knew that I really had some issues understanding geometric proofs, and he would meet me before school every Wednesday for tutoring.

Mr. Howe even helped to preserve my educational reputation as "one of the smart black dudes" by not exposing my need for extra help and having me meet him in his tiny office that was in the main office. And when I say tiny, I mean tiny. The office was only big enough for a student-sized desk and his chair. We had to pull my chair from somewhere in the hallway, and we would share his desk, and he would help me understand when to apply the Pythagorean theorem, side-angle-side rule, and some of those other steps that I still don't completely understand. As a matter of fact, I think he just gave me the D based on effort, and maybe because he knew my family since he taught my sisters. He knew I had the ability, but I just didn't understand this one very important aspect of Geometry. Still, he went that extra mile, which was something Mrs. O'Bannon was not willing to do.

In looking back on my seventh period Advanced Algebra II class, a few things contributed to my lack of success. The first was probably the makeup of the class. I had several of my friends from upper grades in the class. Remember, I was on the "advanced" Math track, and had several seniors that were in the class, that I thought were cool and funny. My man Ksaan Brown was in the class, and his girlfriend Angel, and Chuckie Harris. Ksaan would always say that we made him feel stupid because he was a senior that was taking classes with sophomores. We would always joke him and let him know that he wasn't stupid, we were just smart, and that he would probably end up working for us one day. The sad part was that all of us, as black students, sat in the back corner together. Mrs. O'Bannon liked it that way. As a matter of fact, she created a seating chart for the entire class to prevent some of the extra talking, laughing, and passing notes that would occur in the class. When she created this seating chart, everyone else's seats moved except for ours. She had all the black kids still sitting together, and of course most us were failing, or close to it. I tried the same formula with Mrs. O'Bannon that I did with Mr. Howe. Read the next section the night before, try to get tutoring, make corrections on my quizzes and tests. It didn't really make a difference. When I asked Mrs. O'Bannon about tutoring, she quickly referred me to the National Honor Society Students who were all in her third period Advanced Algebra II class, and that I should try to get up with them after school. I didn't even know who these kids were, and how was I supposed to meet up with them to talk about it if I had French during third period while they were in Math. I would have continued to struggle even more if my mother wouldn't have contacted Mrs. O'Bannon and asked her to help her son in any way she could. There were a few tutoring sessions that would occur after that, but the key concepts just would not sink in. Mrs. O'Bannon always tutored me with the door open so that the whole world could see too.

The second issue with the class was that Mrs. O'Bannon only used direct instruction, and only taught to the front row students. These students always put their hands up to answer questions, and they always got their graded papers back first. I mention this because Mrs. O'Bannon was infamous for waiting until the end of the class period to hand back any graded assignments. It was her philosophy that handing back graded papers at the beginning of class caused distractions for the rest of our 50-minute class period. The bell would ring and then she would always say, like she just remembered "Oh, I have your quizzes, let me pass them out to you." There were several times when I would almost miss getting on the bus because I would get my quiz back last, or next to last. This is probably how Ksaan and I became such good friends because he would have to take me home sometimes because we would be the last two to get back our papers. It took only a few "returning of the papers" for us to realize that she passed her papers out based on your score. So, if you got your paper back early in the distribution, you probably got an A or a B. If you got your paper back late in the distribution, you more than likely got a D or an F. One time I studied for an entire week for an upcoming test, that I thought I had a pretty good handle on, since I had done pretty well on the quizzes leading up to it. On Friday, Mrs. O'Bannon passed back the test, and held mine to last. Before she handed it to me, she stopped, looked at me and said, I am just shocked that you got this, and then handed me my test with "98/A" on it. I was so happy. Here response was, I knew you could do it. What she didn't know is that both of my parents had been working with me all week from 7 p.m. to 9 p.m. to get me prepared. Also, if I didn't do well, they were going to pull me off the basketball team, so you know I was motivated. I missed the bus that day, but luckily, I caught Ksaan as he was leaving the parking lot. I think I got in the way of something that he had planned, because Angel was in the car too.

The final issue with the class was that Mrs. O'Bannon made no effort to relate to "all" of the students in her classes. I believe she was a teacher who was used to working with advanced students only, as she also taught pre-calculus and trigonometry. If we asked a question, that she felt was unworthy, she would usually respond with "I think I have already went over that," or "You should have been paying better attention." These responses usually were met with us putting her down under our breaths and having the entire back half of the class falling out in laughter. She would then say, "What is so funny?" Or she would follow up with the traditional teacher threat of "You won't think this is so funny when you see your grades." Wow, what a statement to a group of students. Now I bring these issues up with Mrs. O'Bannon because she is the only class I have ever failed in my life. It was devastating. My parents even discussed me going to summer school and taking the class over. Summer school? No! Give up my summer jobs? Being in classes with people I knew I was smarter than? Getting up early? No! Finally, I convinced my parents to just let me take the class again in the fall. And I did, and I got an A. I guess I should have earned an A because it was my second time taking the class, but it was also because I had a teacher who cared about her students and took the time to re-explain things. Failing my Advanced Algebra II class was a humbling experience that taught me to be prepared and do everything that I can to be successful. I applied this motivation to my years at the University of Virginia, and one day when I came back to Hermitage for homecoming because my girlfriend at the time was a year younger than me, I happened to bump into Mrs. O'Bannon in the commons area. She did the typical, "How is school?" What are you majoring in?" type of questions, and as she exited our conversation, she said, "You know, I am glad that you failed my class. I was hoping it would help you in the long run." I could not believe she said that. Who tells someone that? All I could think of was that she had to hurry away because her broom and spells were waiting for her back in her classroom.

I tell this story so that our current teachers will know what not to do. I made sure when I became a teacher, I took the time to get to know my students. I made sure that I used a variety of instructional strategies during my instruction so that each student could show their strengths. I kept the horror tales of Mrs. O'Bannon in the back of my mind anytime I felt that I was not reaching a certain student or a group of students. When I became an administrator, I always preached to the faculty/staff how important it was to build relationships with students, use their interests as part of the foundation for instruction, and to develop student buy-in within the lesson. These tips would help with class-room management, overall active engagement, and would generally have students developing a desire to "want" to attend your class. I know that many teachers of today may find this difficult due to the high levels of accountability that is present in education today.

One of the hardest parts of being a teacher who wants to build relationships with students is to make sure they are not perceived as a "friend." This is always difficult with new or younger teachers who might be fresh out of college, meaning they are closer to the age of the students they instruct, especially if they are teaching at the secondary level. The idea of being the cool teacher is something that all teachers want deep down, but having their respect instead of having them like you is of greater importance. I always wanted to be the respected teacher who just so happened to be the coolest teacher they knew. This usually would come with the students sometimes sharing a little too much, forgetting that you are around and using profanity (I taught in a high school for ten years), and knowing when you put your foot down or enforce a rule. The class and sometimes the parents would completely understand why I had to take the stance that I did. It didn't hurt that I was also the basketball coach, which always meant an extra amount of respect in the building, an extra notch or two on the coolness scale, and being under the microscope for everything that I did.

Teachers today must wear many hats. This includes being the father/mother figure, the mentor, the role model, you name it. Teachers today must understand that you are shaping lives for the years to come and it is very important that teachers understand that the impressions they make will last a long time. I am sure you are reflecting on your favorite teacher right now. What made that teacher so special to you? Was it the fact that they gave the best treats and snacks around the holidays? Was it their sense of humor? Was it the fact that this teacher took the time to get to know you on a more personal level? Or was it just because this teacher was a good instructor? You know the answers to these questions. I think one of the biggest compliments that was ever given to me by one of my former students is that they could still remember a lot of the facts that I taught them in my World History II class. Of course, they remembered the *Star Wars* movies that I used as a metaphor for the Holocaust, but they also remembered how World War I started, and the key players in that conflict. That and the fact that they told their parents to make sure their younger siblings also had me as a teacher. Those are the moments that make you feel good.

Chapter 3

Teacher Reflections

Listed below are ten characteristics that are widely accepted as being strong qualities of a good teacher. Please rank them from one to ten, with one being the most important, and ten being the least important. Please discuss your top and bottom three qualities in your book groups, or with other colleagues at your earliest convenience.

_____ Ability to be Flexible

_____ Building Relationships

_____ Classroom Management

_____ Communication Skills

_____ Having High Expectations

_____ Knowledge of the Subject Matter

_____ Knowledge of their Students

_____ Organization Skills

_____ Professionalism

_____ Years of Experience

This is probably one of the proudest pictures of my life. Not only did I make the team, but I started at shooting guard and was a captain. I think this is where Air Gordon was born!

Chapter 4

The Leader

My mother always told me that I was a leader. At first, I thought she was only saying these things because all parents provide their kids with the same message of being a leader and not being a follower. Growing up with my friends, Titus, Jamal, Will, and Shawn, I was characterized as the leader of our little crew because I was the oldest. Really, I was only two weeks older than Titus, but he would say I was the leader because he didn't want to deal with the craziness of making plans to do something if he didn't have too. I also don't think that he wanted the responsibility of being held accountable if our plans did not work out. I think that leadership is relative depending on the group that is being assembled. When I was hanging with Tony Wood or Darin Johnson, I wasn't considered the leader because they were two and five years older than me. I know what you are thinking. What was I doing hanging with people who were that much older than me, especially in Darin's case? I think one of the reasons could be that besides looking up to these guys because they were great athletes, great with the ladies (which, as we know, are the two most important things for every pre-teen and teenage boy), and they just seemed to be right about a lot of things. I figured that because they were older and we all grew up in the same neighborhood, we all made the same mistakes. My adolescent logic led me to believe that I should listen to these guys and take their advice so that I don't make the same mistakes.

When I got to high school, I think my leadership ability began to really show. Some of it had to do with the confidence that I had because I was finally on the basketball team, I still had good grades, and was perceived to be on the right track for success. Being the captain of the basketball team every year in high school was a big deal to me. Not only did I like the recognition of standing at half court and talking to the officials so that everyone knew I was special, but also because it let me know that my coaches viewed me as one of the better players and trusted me to make the right decisions and be the voice for the team. When your boss, coach, or in many cases peers choose you as a leader, it carries a lot of weight for your self-esteem and ego. I think the leadership position of being a captain on the ninth-grade basketball team was so special because that position was chosen by my teammates. Remember, this was my first year of playing with them, since many of them played together on the middle school team that I was cut from for two years. (Damn you, Coach Madison!) It meant that I had their respect and that they knew I was the right person for the title.

Being a captain led to me having the confidence to join other clubs and hold office. I figured that I was popular enough, smart enough, and knew enough people that I could get their support. At first, I was still a little hesitant because of what happened when I ran for eighth grade class president at Brookland Middle School. I have already mentioned how I got cut from the basketball team during my sixth and seventh grade years, but I did not try out in the eighth grade. I figured that I would not give Coach Madison the joy of cutting me all three years, especially when I knew that I was good enough to make the team. In my eighth grade year, I decided to try my luck at politics. Word began to spread that there were not any guys running for any of the offices. I already had some experience of being class treasurer when I was in the fifth grade, so a lot of my boys convinced me to run for office so that they could have one of their own in power. We really thought that we were grown and that our decisions could really change the school. I decided to run for president. I figured if I was going to do it, I was going to make sure that I was in charge. I submitted all my paperwork, had good teacher recommendations, and I even had a campaign manager in Valeta Sutton. I was ready to go. However, the teachers did not choose me to be on the ballot. I still do not know why. I was more-angry than upset, but it was something that makes you pause and reflect. Maybe I was not as popular as I thought I was. Maybe they saved me from some embarrassment as there was a chance that I was not going to win anyway. When the results were released from the election, Kamala Brooks had won, and Sunday Tinnell got second. In our election, whoever got second, was automatically named the vice president. What is more interesting, is that I got third, with write-ins only. Kamala credited me for her being president because I told everyone to vote for her since I was not on the ballot. I had no idea that I was going to get a lot of write-in votes and even beat out the other two candidates that were on the ballot. I guess a lot of my friends were serious about giving me their support.

Now I am not going to lie and tell you that I won every office I ran for, as I can remember being reminded that I was not as popular as I thought I was when I ran for Key Club vice president. I had been in Key Club for a year and I was going to try to follow the formula of being in a club for a year and then holding office the second year, and then if you are successful at those steps, becoming President the following year. Well in this Key Club election, I was quickly reminded that I was not in as tight with this group as I thought. Many of the members had been in Key Club together since their freshman year, and I had joined as a sophomore. They followed the pecking order of the senior members being the individuals who should hold the leadership positions. I lost the election, which only took five minutes to tally the votes. I lost to Steve Smith, who also is one of my closest friends, and had encouraged me to join the Key Club with him as a freshman. I wasn't mad but was a little disappointed. And to add insult to injury, the members asked me to give Steve's acceptance speech, because along with Baxton and Titus, he and I had created this new type of slang that everyone was now starting to use. They thought it was hilarious the way we substituted words like "what's up" and "How you doing?" with "Fied" and "Green." I told you, we were very influential on others during our high school careers, so much that we created our own dialect and had almost the entire school using new slang that we made up one day at Steve's house.

Fast forward to my senior year of high school. The teachers held me in high regard until they found out that my girlfriend Katrina was pregnant. Now remember, this was the early 1990s, and teenage pregnancy was very new and even more taboo than it is right now. Our situation was a little different, because Katrina and I both came from good homes, and had supportive parents, and of course we thought we were in love. At the time, I think Katrina was the only girl at Hermitage who was pregnant. Everyone knew. Teachers, the administration, custodians, parents, and of course the fans from the rival schools who would now heckle me during basketball games. To experience this at seventeen was really tough.

To make matters worse, or more complicated, Katrina's father was a preacher. He banned us from seeing each other. We had a run-in at Safeway over the summer when I had won a big stuffed animal at King's Dominion on one of those basketball shooting games, and I brought the stuffed animal to her job to surprise her. Teenage love. As fate would have it, when Titus, Jamal, Will, Shawn, and I pulled up, so did her father. He basically told us that we could not be there. My boys, who never backed down from anything, reminded him that this was a public place and that he could not dictate where we could go. Things of course went downhill from there.

When all these people found out that I impregnated the preacher's daughter, I no longer was the guy who parents wanted their daughters to date. I no longer was the guy who moms wanted their daughters to be escorted to the debutante ball, to dances, or anything. I think they had the fear that if I looked at their daughters, their daughters would automatically become pregnant. I can remember having the conversation with my mother that no one would date me anymore. I could tell by the way that my mom looked at me that she was really hurt by the way I was feeling. Now, it wasn't like I no longer was going to have any success with the girls, but it hurt that their parents no longer viewed me as a catch, or someone who was going to be successful.

The first family that kind of treated me this way was Vikki Atwater's. Her mom did a complete 180 when she found out that I had a son. Before she received this information from one of her girlfriends, Vikki and I were doing fine. It was one of my first long-distance relationships, since I was off to college for my first year at the University of Virginia. Vikki was a year younger than me, so she was a senior at Hermitage High School. At first, her mother thought that everything was great because she knew my family, which meant I came from good stock, as my parents used to call it. I was attending one of the best universities in the country, and I had shared with her my aspiration of becoming a physical therapist for either a professional sports team or somewhere at the college level. I had the entire thing mapped out. But then Mrs. Atwater received that phone call. I can remember Vikki calling me. She was so upset and telling me that her parents did not want her to see me anymore. I asked her why, and she said that she would rather tell me in person, so I came home that weekend. I went to Vikki's house, and I could tell that she had been crying. She told me that her mom found out that I had a son, and that she did not want her daughter "dating a boy like that." To this day, I am still trying to figure out what "like that" meant. I told Vikki that we could make it because we loved each other, and that we should not let them stop us. Damn. It sounded very similar to the conversation that Katrina and I had had one year before. I could tell that Vikki was willing to try, but right then her father yelled down the steps, "Vikki, it is time for your friend to go." Damn. So now I am your friend, and no longer did I have the name of John. This was the same guy who used to joke with me all the time while praising the fact that I attended a "white school" and was trying to do great things. He always used to say that my car was a "piece of sh*t" and that it better not ever break down with his daughter in the car. Wow, how quickly things turn.

Over the next year or so, Vikki and I would still see each other every now and then, but things were never the same. Her mother really hurt me. Vikki and I were off and on for the next couple of months, but then tried to rekindle things a little bit over the summer. I thought that things were going to work out, but of course, the universe had other plans. I can also remember one day when Vikki was in college, she started to see someone else, but had contacted me to give me back some of my old belongings. I thought it was a little odd, as I could have picked them up at any time, but she insisted that I come over and get them on this particular day. When I went to the door, I heard someone playing the piano. When I rang the doorbell, the playing stopped, and some dude opened the door. He was about my age but looked a lot older in the face. As he let me into the house, Mrs. Atwater came prancing down the steps. I assume that Vikki was up in her room, because she came down a few minutes later. Mrs. Atwater made sure that she introduced me to Vikki's new boyfriend and began bragging on him being a music major and of course his musical exploits throughout the state of North Carolina. I really did not care for any of this information, but it was obvious that she was really getting a kick out of this.

Vikki came downstairs and handed me a shoebox that had many of the items in it that I had given her over the last couple of years. I could tell that she was kind of embarrassed by the theatrics that her mother had just displayed, but she went along with it anyway. I really believed that was a cruel thing for an adult to do, but it let me know that some people can be very vindictive. The funny part is that Vikki and her musically inclined boyfriend did not stay together that long, as it turned out he liked guys. What is even funnier was that in my adult life, I still bump into Mrs. Atwater all the time at the grocery store, and she likes to strike up conversation like we had a very good relationship. She now compliments me on being very successful and how she always liked me. One day last year, I called her out on that and told her that she never liked me, so why would she try to act like she did now? The look on her face was priceless. She told me that if I had loved her daughter, I would have fought for her! I couldn't believe that those words came out of her mouth. And why was she saying this to me twenty years later? When I told my mother this story, she laughed. She said that Mrs. Atwater had probably realized that she had made a mistake because I had become successful in life. My mom said that Mrs. Atwater probably regretted the way she treated me. As usual, I think my mother was right.

In college, leadership usually was based on who was the smartest person in the group, who had the best ideas, or sometimes by default because no one else wanted the responsibility. I was considered one of the leaders on my first-year hall because a lot of the other dudes were very shy. Maybe they were just kind of nerdy and were a little intimidated by this black dude from Richmond. Being from Richmond carried a lot of weight at UVA. I think part of it had to do with the fact that at the time, Richmond was the number one murder capital in the country. Because of some of the poor decisions made by others, being from Richmond gave me automatic street cred, even though my address was smack dab in the middle of the suburbs. I can remember Cory Alexander pointing that out one day when we were all at a cookout, and some dude was listing all the people at UVA from Richmond. When the dude mentioned me, Cory said, "I have been to John's house. Straight suburbs." We all laughed because it was true.

My RA (resident advisor), Mike Royster, would always say that Jim and I were leaders because all the other dudes on our hall looked up to us. For some, it could have been the first two real black dudes that they ever hung with. Some of my leadership was given because I was trying out for the basketball team and guys like Cory Alexander and Junior Burrough would pick me up, drop me off, or better yet, if I was seen eating lunch with them and my hall mates would walk by. The conversation would always get interesting at dinner when my hall mates, Tom Hillman or Dave Donovan, would say "I can't believe you know Cory Alexander, Junior Burrough, or Bryant Stith. It was a big deal, but I tried to play it off, like they had been my boys for life. I had known Cory for about three years, as we played on one of the first AAU basketball programs in the Richmond Metro Area together. Jason Williford was on that team, too, and was on the UVA Basketball team, but Tom, Dave, and Chris did not gawk over him as much because he was not in the rotation our first year. Internally, it was hard hanging around the basketball guys sometimes because I was still just trying out. I went from being one of the best basketball players growing up in my area, to an above-average prospect as a walk-on in the ACC. As I have said before in this chapter, being a leader of a group is relative to the dynamics of the group. When I played with the members of UVA's basketball team from 1991–1993, I could hold my own, but I would still get excited if I scored or made a good play. It was a little different when I played with my hall mates or pick-up games at Slaughter and I would dominate the court. All my life I was known as John Gordon, basketball player, but I soon realized that at UVA I was going to have to reinvent myself as something else.

At the University of Virginia, it is assumed that everyone is smart, graduated in the top 5 percent of their class, and had an unbelievable high school resume. I had almost all those things, except for the graduating in the top 5 percent of their class part. Because I really believed that I was going to play basketball at UVA, I never really thought about joining other groups and organizations until 1993 when I realized that my dream of making the team and dressing for a game were over. For two years, I had practiced almost every day, played on the JV team, which in my opinion was downright embarrassing, and never knowing if I was going to travel or finally get to dress. I can remember us walking through the hall at University Hall aka "U-Hall" and being stopped by security because the women's team was at practice and they wanted to know who we were. Dwayne, our starting power-forward, who could jump out of the gym, but had the ugliest shot in America, proudly told the guy,

"We are the UVA JV Team." I hated the way it sounded. I hadn't played JV since the tenth grade, and all that meant to me was that we were not good enough to play varsity. That was when I knew that I had to make a name for myself in some other way.

I joined the NAACP because there were issues on campus with potential budget cuts that could affect a lot of minority students who were admitted due to affirmative action. I was one of them. We also had some racial issues that occurred that the Black Student Alliance (BSA) felt were not properly handled by President Casteen. In typical black pride power, we marched on the president's office. It was something to see over five hundred African-American students moving through campus in unison, all wearing black armbands, and being extremely quiet. The funny part was watching some of the white students walking down the sidewalk towards us, and then switching to the other side of the street because 500 black people were walking towards them. Now that I think about it, I probably would have done the same thing. Once we arrive at the president's office, the news and media outlets are there and ready for the confrontation. A few of us asked a lot of questions about funding for minority programs, minority scholarships, and the current racial climate. President Casteen gave us some prepared answers but did not speak of any action. As quiet as we came, we walked out in the middle of one of President Casteen's responses. The next day, when the news footage hit, my mother called me because the picture she saw had me in the front row while President Casteen was speaking. It made her think that I was one of the organizers, instead of just being a dude who decided to attend this march instead of going to class. A few others thought that as well, and the next thing you knew, I was receiving emails inquiring about my interest in joining this group or speaking at this rally or cause, all because I was in the right place at the right time.

Being at the right place at the right time can help get your foot in the door, but once you are put into that position, you must make sure you show leadership. While at UVA, I ended up joining the Minority Student Admissions Council, which had the chief responsibility of reviewing applications from potential students. It was our job to complete phone interviews, review high school resumes, and try to get the students to come on tours of the campus. I was interested in this job because it allowed me to look at some of the new girls who might come to UVA. Remember, back then, you had to submit a picture with your application, which was the first and best piece of information that a college guy could have. Most of the students were exceptional educationally, but some seemed to lack the well-rounded student persona that the University of Virginia was looking for.

I thought that most people at UVA at the time were very similar to me, but as you talked to them more, or got to know them better, you began to realize that everyone had a unique story and situation that allowed them to end up in Charlottesville. The interesting part about this phase of my life was that as I got older, the first and second year students were trying to categorize me based on what they had heard: Is he an athlete? Is he an activist? Didn't I just hear him on the radio (WIRE) on Friday night? Didn't he just serve as the master of ceremony (MC) at this party?

I was just doing things that I thought were fun, and of course if it got me some visibility, then it was even better. I realized that I could fit into almost every group, and depending on the topic, I could be considered an expert or a leader in the field. I think this helped me grow, as my interest expanded from just basketball, hip-hop, and girls to racial equality, low levels of political awareness, and god forbid what I was going to do after college. As I switched from being classified as pre-med to a history and finally a psychology major, I realized that I traveled through several different phases while in college. Upon first arrival, it was about basketball, preserving my "street cred," and finding which group I would fit into. Soon it transformed into being a leader of one of my little crews (my suite mates Damian, Glen, Jim, Rupert, and Kevin) while still having exposure to being part of the athletic group that came to school the same year we did. Even though a lot had changed since all of us were in the Summer Transition Program (STP) together, we would still get together and party whenever we could like it was the summer of 1991. But as Junior Burrough and Cory Alexander were beginning to receive contact on their potential draft status in the NBA, I was trying to figure out what type of job I was going to get once we graduated.

I think it became crystal clear when my friend Jim started to talk about whether he could get a job with AMS, since he knew they paid more than some of the other offers that he received. Jim was graduating from the McIntire School of Commerce, and he was being recruited by several companies in the Northern Virginia area. I then realized that as a psychology major, I wasn't really being recruited by anyone. Jim accepted the offer to work at AMS, and then during several conversations with others, I began to hear more and more people settling in on their first professional opportunities out of college. I did not want to be the guy who was going to have to move back home, especially with a degree from UVA. That was exactly what my father wanted me to do, because my sisters had done so when they graduated. Of course, they moved back home because they were transitioning into graduate school. What my father did not know was that they had private talks with me about wishing they had not moved back home. They would complain about how they no longer had the privacy and freedom that they had in school, and that it seemed that their father (who was recently retired) would always be in their business. This is probably the reason why, when Donna started medical school, she quickly got an apartment on the other side of Richmond. Their warnings stuck in my head for years, and I promised that I would not make the same mistake.

As Shavonne finalized her first job with DuPont, mainly because they were going to pay her $40,000 and provide her with a relocation package, I realized the clock was ticking. I had two offers upon graduation, both in the field of insurance. Life of Virginia offered me $3,000 as a signing bonus and instructed me to use the money to get my own place and to purchase a computer to document which of my recent college graduate friends would be willing to purchase insurance. New York Life offered me a job mainly because of my father having a conversation with Mr. Joel Cohen and basically asking him to give his son a job. When I went on my interview with New York Life, I met with some very rich guy in a huge office. He explained to me that he believed that I could make a lot of money in the business, but that I would have to grow my clientele. Clientele? I didn't have any clientele. He then suggested that I contact my college graduate friends and try to sell them life insurance. Now, I knew that many of my college friends were just setting up their own budgets and had no concept of purchasing insurance, mainly because they could not afford it. He explained that I was going to have to take several tests to get my series six and seven licenses so that I could sell insurance and mutual funds. I didn't know that working in the insurance industry was going to be so hard. He also suggested that I live at home for a year because I wasn't going to make any "real money" in the first year. This was when he gave me the bottom line: if you don't sell policies or get people to commit, you won't make any money. All I can remember is him saying that I would get paid on commission from blah, blah ... commission? That was when I heard my mother's voice reminding me to never take a job based on commission because I wouldn't have a steady income. Salary. Yes, salary. That was what I wanted.

I remember coming home and telling my father that I wasn't going to take either job, and that I was going to move to Salisbury, Maryland with Shavonne and go into the field of education. I knew I could get a job as a substitute teacher, and maybe something else. I really didn't have a plan; I just knew that I did not want to live at home, nor did I go to school for four years at UVA only to come out and sell insurance. I also figured that maybe I could coach basketball and use that as the motivator to teach. It was a thought.

Chapter 4

Leadership Reflections

1) In your own words, describe what you feel are the top three characteristics of being a leader.

2) Can leadership be taught or is it something that is internal? Or is it both?

3) How do you think we should promote leadership in school?

4) Should we have the same expectations of leadership in adults and in children?

Chapter 5

The Coach

I never really thought about becoming a coach until my first year at UVA, when my college roommate Scott asked me if I would be interested in coaching him and our hall mate Austin for their fraternity intramural team. I can remember standing on the sideline for the first time and yelling out general instructions such as "help-side" and "back off him because he can't shoot" and just trying to find the mismatch on the floor at the offensive end. Remember, I was more influenced by the NBA game which was all about finding the mismatch, forcing the defense to double-team or trap, and then swinging the ball to the open man or open shot. As I really got into it, I can also remember Jim, being the comedian that he was, pulling down my white sweatpants as I stood on the sideline. He pantsed me. Luckily, I had on some basketball shorts underneath, or I would have made my coaching debut in my tighty-whities. I got a rush out of coaching that day, and that was probably when I changed my thought process and dreams to maybe trying to make it to the NBA as a coach now instead of as a player. Or maybe I could become the head coach at the University of Virginia. I think the biggest kick that I get out of coaching is when you say exactly the right thing and the players on the floor execute and it works out perfectly. Both games that I coached for Scott's fraternity team ended in victory. I didn't really coach any more games at UVA, but it did help me see the game a little differently when I played from that point forward.

When Shavonne and I moved to Salisbury, Maryland, it was a new experience for me. I had one college friend, Brandon Barkley, who lived in the area. He helped to show me around town. Brandon gave me a lot of insight into how many of his friends that he had gone to high school with still lived in the area, but really were not doing anything with their lives. He told me how some of his boys had been locked up, some had recently gotten out of jail, and how even more were on drugs or were selling drugs: sad stories. Brandon described the area as having a lot of potential and that there were a lot of good people, but many of them were never given the opportunity to make their lives better. I told Brandon that I wanted to become a teacher and a basketball coach, but in the meantime, I just wanted to go out to play some ball and have a little fun. One of the more interesting things about Salisbury is that the adults played basketball religiously every day after work at 6 p.m. Brandon said that the majority of the "successful" people who were doing anything with their lives would all get off from their shift at one of the factories at 5 p.m. They would change their clothes at the playground or go home real quick to be ready for the games at 6 p.m. Some of the guys thought they were good but weren't. When Brandon and I got picked up to play, I think everyone was trying to

walking around Salisbury, and they would ask me if I was hooping today. Of course, I would say yes, and the next thing you know, I had a lot of new friends and associates. The legend of Virginia spread when we were playing on a Thursday evening and it was the last game of the night. I am not sure if I have mentioned that there were a lot of guys who you could tell were great athletes but who may not have been the most skilled. Some of them obviously were heavy into lifting weights, as having a membership at the local YMCA was like belonging to a prestigious country club.

On this evening, I received the pass in transition and made a move past one of the two defenders that were sprinting back on defense. It ended up being me and one muscle-bound guy who I wanted to make sure didn't foul me so hard that I would end up missing work as a substitute teacher the next day. Remember, I was waiting on calls from either Somerset County (primarily Washington HS) or Wicomico County every morning so that I could earn a living. Missing a day meant I could not pay my share of the bills. Well, this guy seemed to be a little clumsy on his feet, since he was backpedaling real hard. I dribbled right at him when he was at the foul line. I hesitated, faked like I was going right, and then threw the ball off the backboard as I moved past him on his left. As he turned around to see where the ball went, I jumped, caught the ball in mid-air, and dunked it with two hands! All three games that were happening on the courts stopped. The crowd went crazy. Some dudes started to yell, "Oh! Oh [you may insert any curse word here that you would like]!" as they grabbed their keys, kids, and whatever else was close by as they ran to my court. Now what a lot of people did not know, is that I have done that move dozens of times on the court. But this was the first time the playground legends in Salisbury had seen anything like that before.

My reputation as an outstanding basketball player grew by leaps and bounds over the next couple of months. My next haircut at the barbershop was free, because my barber Marvin Church explained to me that I was "real" and that a lot of the dudes around here were "wack" and that he and I need to hang together more often. I was asked to host a basketball camp for the Wicomico County Parks and Recreation Department, because Brian, the parks and recreation supervisor, wanted to have a basketball camp but he felt that he did not have a big enough name to get the camp going. His wife Karen and Shavonne both worked together for DuPont, and I think Shavonne recommended me. I was so excited to have my own camp. The advertisement said, "Former Virginia standout, John Gordon would be the organizer and teach the kids about basketball in the Atlantic Coast Conference (ACC)." Former basketball standout? I laughed, but Brian said it was the best way to get the parents to pay for the camp, and he was right. In organizing the camp, I set up the traditional stations of ball-handling, shooting, defense, rebounding, etc. I really just emulated the set-up from all the camps that I had attended at William and Mary, Randolph-Macon, Five-Star, and so on from my middle and high school career. The camp had about thirty kids, and I brought in Jamal Robinson, who was the starting shooting guard at UVA at the time, as the guest speaker. Jamal was so exciting to watch and is really a good guy. He was honored to speak at my first camp, and of course we played some pick-up games at the University of Maryland

Eastern-Shore later that evening. I still stay in touch with him today, and he has had a couple of tryouts with some NBA teams, but has thrived playing overseas. The local paper covered the basketball camp mainly because Jamal was there. This exposure helped my reputation as a strong basketball mind, and the following year, I had about fifty kids attend the camp. I could definitely see my coaching career getting started in a great way.

As I was making my living as a substitute teacher, I had interest from both Washington High School and Mardela Middle and High School as an assistant basketball coach. I originally was going to coach at Washington High, but the position was voluntary. At the time they did not have any money in their athletic budget to pay for an assistant coach. The head coach, Mike, was a really nice guy who thought I could help develop the players because they respected me so much. Two weeks before the season started, I got a call from Coach Russell Springman at Mardela Middle and High School, as he had an opening on his staff that was a paid position. I had to take it as I was only making $50 per day as a substitute in Wicomico County and $40 per day as a substitute in Somerset County. The $1000 he offered to be his assistant was something that I could not turn down. My only request was that since I was going to be his assistant, that I would like to be in the building as much as possible. This would be my way to have a steady income as a substitute, but also to help him look after the members of the team. The talent at Mardela was low, especially compared to the athletes that I had two weeks prior at Washington High. At the time, Mardela was known more for their girls' basketball program, because of Rasheedah.

She was a 5'8"-inch guard that was faster than everyone, could shoot, and was very aggressive. I think the year before I got there, the girls team had a record of 20-2, while the boys team was the exact opposite at 2-20. We were bad, but we had some young guards that could make a difference.

Now Mardela Middle and High School was really small. Think about it, the name of the school let you know that the building spanned grades 6-12. Out of those seven grades however, the total enrollment was about five hundred students. When you have a population that small, your talent pool will be thin. But Rashaad and John, the two guards, were really good. Rashaad was a tremendous athlete that could jump out of the gym. He looked a little bit like me physically but could not shoot. He was a senior that realized that he wanted to go to college, but he would not be able to qualify because his grades were too low. Coach Springman already had a plan to send him to junior college because he had some friends that were head coaches at that level. John was a freshman, and he was fast. I mean really fast. As we all know in sports, speed kills, and it is something that cannot be taught. John was still learning the game, but he had older brothers that exposed him to some things that were both positive and negative. He also was a ladies' man, and his reputation grew because he was a freshman starting on the varsity. These two guys, and a forward nicknamed "DT" were basically all we had. In practice, we would have to split Rashaad and John up or Coach Springman and I would have to join in just to make things competitive.

I learned so much from Coach Springman, who played basketball locally at Salisbury State University. I honestly believe that he had a drill to improve every aspect of the game of basketball. He had a lot of energy and fire, and even though he knew we weren't going to win a lot of games, he wanted to make sure the kids were competitive every night. In our first game of the season, Rashaad's cousins were in attendance, and some of them knew me from the basketball courts. We were playing Wicomico High School, or "WI-HI," as they were called. WI-HI was the best basketball team in the area, and they had athletes on their team from one to ten. They would press you the entire game, and they always had good guards and shooters. They were beating us pretty good when I could hear the fans behind us calling my name and telling me to help Rashaad get a dunk. I turned around to acknowledge them and Coach Springman gave me a dirty look and told me not to talk to the people in the stands. He was right. I forgot that I was no longer a player and had to model how we wanted our team to act. He reminded me that we were a team that wasn't winning a lot of games and because both of us were usually on the referees (who were awful by the way) a lot, that we had to be careful. He did not want the reputation of those two young guys at Mardela creating more bad than good with their courtside demeanor. A valuable lesson learned.

The following year, Coach Springman let me know that he aspired of coaching at the collegiate level. I had just gotten my first job at East Salisbury Elementary School as a fifth grade teacher and aspired of becoming a head coach at the high school level. I was very interested in succeeding Coach Springman, but Mardela did not have a teaching vacancy in their social studies department. I also had become close with Coach Terry Gillian at Parkside High School, as he also worked for Parks and Recreation in the

It was so important to see the neighborhoods that our students came from in order to understand some of the trauma that they experienced. This definitely was an eye-opening experience for me.

summer months. That summer, he had talked to me about joining his staff and maybe succeeding him as he did not see himself coaching much longer because he was eyeing retirement. Parkside High School had some athletes as several of their players were at the parks and recreation summer camps and showed how high they could jump and how fast they could run. I figured there were plenty more players at the school that could do the same thing. It also didn't hurt that Parkside was closer to my job at East Salisbury Elementary than Mardela Middle and High.

Coach Terry Gillian was a strong disciplinarian. He was also kind of intimidating as he was also the current head football coach, and a former football player. Judging by the size of him, I would guess that he would have played line-backer at some point and time during his career. Coach Gillian made his number one rule very clear, his way or the highway. I appreciated his disciplinary tactics, and he was big on having his players run for disrespect, not wearing a tie on game days, having poor grades, etc. If a player was talking while he was talking or giving instructions, he would just look at them, and they would automatically drop and give him twenty push-ups. It was amazing to see. I think some of the guys had already been pre-programmed to his disciplinary strategies due to also being on the football team. Parkside High School was a good mixture of African-American and white students. We had good depth on the team including solid guards, strong forwards, and shot blockers on the inside. We also had a junior varsity program that had some talent that probably could have contributed on the varsity. Coach Gillian believed in running the "flex" offense where everyone can score from the elbow or on the back-pick under the basket. Versus the zone, he believed in overloading one side of the floor, meaning to put more offensive players in an area than the defense could cover. Everything looked good on paper, until we played the infamous WI-HI.

They destroyed us. I think the final score was 90-58 or something at that blow-out level. What made matters worse as the game went on, Coach Gillian never made any adjustments. He just continued to sit down and tell the players that they were not playing hard enough, or that they did not run the play correctly or box out, etc. At some point, you would think that he would realize that the system or game plan did not work, and that as a coaching staff we needed to make a few changes. Didn't happen. As the season wore on and we were losing more games than we won, a player revolt occurred. I had enjoyed parts of the games and practices because Coach Gillian allowed me to run the team. I developed the practice plans, and because Coach Gillian liked to sit during the games, I could get-up and pace the sidelines like I was in charge. That was of course until we received several bad calls, because as I said previously, the officiating in this region was awful. And I mean awful. By the time Coach Gillian would get up and argue a call, the referee had already heard enough from me telling him "to run the floor," or "trust his partner" because calls were being made by officials that were out of position. Coach Gillian would receive a technical foul, and then point to me and say, "You got me that technical foul, Mr. Gordon." After a few more games, he would let me stand up for a little while, and then he would slap the chair or the bleachers and sternly say, "Sit down, Mr. Gordon." Meanwhile, we would be losing the game by twenty points.

About halfway through the season, the players had had enough. They talked their parents into going to the principal and letting him know that they no longer wanted to play for Coach Gillian and wanted me to be their coach. I did not know what to say. They said that he was out of touch and did not want to change and kept running the same plays that did not work. I tried to tell the players to be patient and that we would find a way to open-up things in the transition game, and that if we played good defense, everything would take care of itself. The next thing you know, our best player, Gary, quit the team at home, in front of everybody. When he was subbed out of the game for what Coach Gillian thought was a bad shot, he calmly took his jersey off, left it on the bench, and walked to the locker room. His brother, Dante, who was a freshman, witnessed all of this. We had just moved him up to varsity because he was dominating the junior varsity. I can remember his dad saying to me after the game as I was trying to convince him that his son had just made a terrible mistake, "It doesn't matter, because I am going to pull Dante off the team, too."

Damn. Again, I did not know what to say. The next game, our starting center Kyree had gotten into foul trouble, and Coach Gillian took him out of the game. By the time Kyree had checked back in and we were down, he of course was trying to boost his stats and took some ill-advised shots. Coach Gillian benched him for the next game, and when it came time to play WI-HI again, Kyree had also quit the team. WI-HI beat us so bad that game that they doubled our score. Now to be honest, it was a little different when two African-American students had quit the team, and people painted the picture that they were selfish and had discipline problems, but when two white players who also happened to be honor roll students and captains of the football and baseball teams quit the team the following week, then all of a sudden the issues on the team got everyone's attention. I don't really know what happened, but I think Coach Gillian was asked to resign at the end of the season. Either that, or he retired.

When I got my first chance to be a head coach at any level, I tried to take parts of what I had learned from both Coach Springman and Coach Gillian. I wanted to make sure that I covered the skill development piece that Coach Springman had done such a tremendous job. I also liked how he made sure to focus on player development and I admired how he had such a strong relationship with his players. I can honestly say that they trusted him. From Coach Gillian, I also wanted to make sure that I had a strong discipline system in which the players knew the expectations and that parents would appreciate how I was trying to develop bright young men. However, I did not want the players to resent what I was trying to teach them, or have the parents no longer believing in my system or in me as a coach. That is a coach's worse nightmare, which leads to revolt. The sad part about having both of those guys as my first two coaching mentors meant that I did not have a lot of experience in winning as a coach. I had to go back to my Hermitage days and use some of the things I learned from Coach A. C. Little, who served as both my ninth grade and junior varsity coach, and Coach Darryl Jenkins, who served as my varsity coach during my eleventh and twelfth grade year. I won in high school as a player, so now I had to develop ways to create a winning attitude during my first year as a junior varsity coach at Armstrong High School.

I walked into a very political basketball situation at Armstrong High School. Home of the Mighty Wildcats. Mr. Gerry Howard, Principal, made it very clear that we were the Mighty Wildcats. Even though he knew my family very well, he made sure to remind me of the athletic and specifically the basketball history that had come through Armstrong. One of their legendary basketball coaches, Walter Penny, had just retired but was still in the building as a part of a retirement incentive program. His assistant and junior varsity coach Jason Clemons was given the title of interim head coach. He basically had a year to prove that he deserved the job full time. Coach Clemons was a really nice guy who loved the kids. He would do anything for them, and in many cases taught their parents, aunts, brothers and sisters—you name it. In many ways, he was entrenched in the Armstrong family. I am unsure what happened in the relationship with Mr. Howard and Coach Clemons, but it was professional and that was it. I know there were others who reminded me to make sure I remembered that I was a teacher first and a coach second. To me it was all about which one paid the bills. The players liked Coach Clemons as a person but did not respect him as a coach. They would not do anything to blatantly break the rules or be disrespectful to his face, but they knew that he did not know enough about basketball to adjust, draw plays, etc. I picked up on this the first time I went to an open gym shortly after I was hired. Some of the kids would joke about it in between games.

Coach Clemons had been named earlier that summer as the interim boys' basketball coach. He had already picked his staff and was moving forward as one of the regional favorites. We had an All-Metro Guard in Kennard Wyche that could do it all. He and I had several one on one matchups during open gyms and drills, and he was the real deal. Everyone respected his game and they also respected him as a person. We had several other players that were good role players and were ready for the season. Coach Clemons had Coach Kelly Church as his assistant. Coach Church was a student of the game but was a little over the top in his antics. However, as a basketball mind he is one of the best. He ran practices, ran the games, did it all so Coach Clemons would not fail. Coach Church was motivated in facing Atlee High School, where he had coached previously and had recently resigned. He wanted to stick it to Atlee twice a year.

He also had Coach Mike Wilson as his junior varsity coach. Coach Wilson was an east end of Henrico developmental coaching legend. I think he coached both boys' and girls' basketball at almost every middle and high school in Eastern Henrico and the City of Richmond. Coach Clemons told me that I was going to be his assistant. However, Mr. Howard wanted me to be the junior varsity head coach because I taught in the building. This was the start of some political drama. Because Mr. Howard, and Mr. Samuels, our athletic director, had the final say, Coach Clemons did not have a choice. I was promoted to junior varsity coach before I even started teaching. This made the situation a little uncomfortable for Coach Clemons and me. I think it made him not trust me fully, and I didn't blame him. We all got along very well, and there were a lot of good basketball minds on our staff, but Coach Clemons wanted to create this façade, mainly for me, that he was the "brains" behind everything, even though we all knew it was Coach Church. I will never forget at our first or second coaches meeting, Coach Clemons stopped the meeting and pulled Coach Church into the kitchen, which had no door to block out the sound. He reminded Coach Church that in front of me, he must make all the decisions and suggestions and it can't come from him. One of the craziest and most awkward things I had ever heard.

Coach Clemons figured that if I did not have a successful junior varsity season, then there would not be any way that I would beat him out and become varsity coach the next year. He did what a lot of head coaches did, he moved all the talent, regardless of grade level, to the varsity. It made practice more competitive, but it angered some of the parents and players because their children were not getting any playing time during the games. Coach Clemons played seven or eight guys and leaned on the seniors a lot. Meanwhile, this was my first head coaching assignment, so I already had plays in mind, and I knew how I wanted my team to look. I had studied all the colleges and universities that had cats, lions, and tigers (oh my) to develop some warm-up shirt and uniform designs. If the players look good, then they will play good. I believed this, and I knew that my players would love the fact that they looked like their favorite schools. We had navy-blue Nike t-shirts with their last name and a paw print on the back, and a capital A on the front. Our warm-up package, with the shoes and socks, looked better than the varsity. Mr. Howard and Mr. Samuels gave me permission to fundraise. When I spoke to Coach Clemons about it, he told me that the varsity would do their own thing. He did not leave me with a lot of support on certain issues, and I understood why.

Then when the junior varsity started to win games, and looked good doing it, Coach Clemons informed me that he was moving my starting guards up to the varsity for the next game. As I have stated before, in basketball, if you don't have good guards, you don't win. Period. I couldn't believe this was happening, but I had to remember that I was set up to fail. On the other end, Coach Clemons and Coach Church were beginning to disagree about more and more things in public. Coach Clemons did not like how the players were going to Coach Church with questions, and he felt that Coach Church overstepped and dismissed him sometimes. Especially during games. Coach Church felt like nothing had changed since they agreed to work together in the summer. He thought that Coach Clemons was threatened by him and me when all we were trying to do is win. Coach Church had enough and quit one day after practice. It wasn't pretty, but it sent shockwaves through the locker room. He called me that night and said that he couldn't do it anymore and that he wanted to spend more time with his kids. He still attended a lot of our games after he quit.

The question of how the JV would respond to losing the starting backcourt, and how the program would go on without Coach Church was secondary to a string of games coming up in the varsity schedule that would shape the near basketball future of Armstrong High School. We were to play Thomas Jefferson, Henrico, and Highland Springs. All three teams were good, but Highland Springs was the talk of the area because they were blowing teams out and started two freshmen guards. Our games had also been moved to 4:30 in the afternoon, with varsity playing first, due to violence that had started at George Wythe and Huguenot High Schools. On the afternoon of playing Thomas Jefferson (Tee-Jay), I noticed that Tee-Jay had only eight players dressed. I pointed this out to Coach Clemons who decided that he was going to try to tire Tee-Jay out by running the entire game. In the pre-game talk, he told the team that we were going to run a 2-2-1 defense and press them the entire game. All the players agreed but the other varsity assistants looked at each other and asked why we were doing this, especially since we had not practiced this all week. Needless to say, we lost the game.

In the post-game meeting, players were fussing at other players, coaches were trying to calm them down, and Coach Clemons was outside talking with parents and reporters. He walked in amongst the chaos and he looked like the weight of the world was on his shoulders. He told everybody that if they should be mad at anyone, then it should be him. He was the head coach. It was his responsibility. At the end of his postgame tirade, he looked at all of us and said, "You guys won't have to worry about this anymore. You won't have to worry about me anymore. Because I resign!" He then stormed out the back of the locker room. Everybody was in shock.

The team mom, Mrs. Hatcher, did a great job of calming everybody down. She said that we had given up on our coach, and that there was a lot of pressure on him. She and I went into the hallway where Coach Clemons was leaning up against the wall, and she began to comfort him. This was tough for me because I wanted to be a head coach and thought that Armstrong would be my best shot at making that happen, but when I looked at Coach Clemons, I knew he was in pain. He snapped out of it quickly when we both suggested that he go back into the locker room and talk to the kids. He agreed. He walked back into the locker room into dead silence. Some of the players had already started to get dressed. He apologized to them and said that he wasn't a quitter. He said all the right things, but it was too late. He had lost the players' respect, and it would never be the same.

We played Highland Springs, which was number one at the time and started two freshmen guards in Jonathan Hargett and Maurice Carter. They were nice. Maurice could

career ended in moments. The only bright spot that night was seeing Benny walk out with only abrasions on his face.

In Kennard's hospital room, he was in great spirits. Unbelievably great. As we all thought about his basketball career in the back of our minds, he talked about how he was lucky to be alive. How he was happy that he only got hit in the knee and not in his heart. This was perspective that I will never forget. He grew up that day right before our eyes. We received a call from Coach Lancaster from Highland Springs. He heard about it only hours after we did. He wanted to check on everyone, was so sad to hear about Kennard, and hoped it was not basketball related. Coach Clemons and I both thanked him for the call. That was a class move that showed the type of man that Coach Lancaster was. However, the shock of what happened to Kennard and his friends was still present. If I remember correctly, Kennard described the event as a misunderstanding about something that was said to someone a while ago. How the shots were fired across the street without warning, and how they could have just been in the wrong place at the wrong time. Kennard talked briefly about playing again, but knew he had a tough road ahead of him. We all believed him but knew that the team would not handle any of this well. There were discussions to cancel the season. We only had to play one or two more games for the rest of the regular season, so Mr. Samuels thought we should finish. He was right, but we had to play Highland Springs again the following week, and it was a numbing feeling to even think about it. We got embarrassed on the court. We looked lost. Everyone understood why. Even though we were a high seed for the tournament based on our regular season record, mentally we wanted the season to be over. We lost in the first round of the district tournament to Lee-Davis and did not make the regional tournament. A disappointing end to what started as such as promising season. Now I see why many of my students would tell me there is such a thing as bad luck.

About a month after the season ended, Mr. Howard and Mr. Samuels informed me that the basketball job was open. Coach Clemons was going to be able to apply for the job full time, just like all the rest of us. For about two or three weeks after the deadline had passed, I kept asking Mr. Samuels when the interviews would begin. He said he was waiting on Mr. Howard because his schedule was so busy. When I would see Mr. Howard, he would always yell at Mr. Samuels and say, "When are we going to do these interviews for boys' basketball?" He would then look at me and smile and say, "I have to hire me a coach, and I am ready to interview by myself if I need to!" It was so funny to see Mr. Samuels and Mr. Howard go back and forth like that. When the interview finally arrived, I was ready. The panel consisted of Mr. Howard, both assistant principals-Mrs. Hester and Mrs. Ward, Mr. Samuels, and Mr. Rakestraw. Mr. Rakestraw served as the academic advisor and statistician for the team. Of course, I counted votes as I sat down and figured that Rakestraw was a big Clemons supporter. However, during the interview when I gave a good response he would smile and wink at me. I think he was trying to help me relax as I know I probably began to talk fast because I had so much to say. I had my portfolio in order with a plan describing events and activities for the pre-season, in-season, and off-season. I had plans for creating a social organization that would better tie the players to the community. The program was called the AWO: Armstrong Wildcat Order. I was a big wrestling fan at the time and patterned the program, which included extensive weight training, study halls, and community service, after the NWO from the old World Championship Wrestling days. The program was backed by Kappa Alpha Psi Fraternity, Inc. as we started a Kappa Guide Right Program to begin in the fall.

I had a plan. I can remember Mrs. Hester leaving the building when I did and telling me how impressed she was with my presentation. It made me feel especially good when she said, "Don't let her down!" I promised her that I would not, and I started to think I was going to get the job. About a week later, Mr. Howard and Mr. Samuels called me into Mr. Howard's office. They told me I had the job. I was so excited that Mr. Howard looked at me and laughed as he told me to sit back down in my chair. They told me that it would become official at the next school board meeting, and that they were informing the unsuccessful candidates in the next few days. Wow. So now I knew that I had the job, but Clemons didn't know that he did not. Over the two weeks that we waited, the Armstrong rumor mill began to circulate that Coach Clemons had gotten the job and I watched him tell people his plans for the team in the hallway and everything. It was hard to watch. He and I both walked downstairs together to go to lunch. As we were walking by the office, one of the secretaries called me into the office because I had a phone call. Coach Clemons told me he would meet me in the cafeteria. On the phone was Coach Kelly Church. He just wanted to congratulate me for

It is only fitting that this picture has me standing beside my bulletin board titled "The Info" as I watch the students work together in World Geography. Also, I knew that community service could help our players get into school and build that high school resume. The A.W.O. or Armstrong Wildcat Order was the modern version of a Varsity Club with a wresting twist. The guys are even showing the "A," "W," and "O" in the pic!

getting the job, even though it had not become official yet. Of course, I had to play dumb, but he told me to "Cut the crap!" He said that Mr. Howard and Mr. Samuels are not stupid. They know they had a good young coach in their building who could lead the program. I thanked him for the kind words and told him I would call him later. As I was hanging up the phone, it happened. Three sharp sounds, like firecrackers going off in the hall.

I remember freezing. Suddenly, kids were ducking and running up the hall. Some of the students were running out of the front of the school and some ran into the office with me. I followed them. I had been in places where you heard gunshots before, but never that close. It was one of the most terrifying experiences of my life. Three of us ran behind the mailroom area. One of the girls ran and locked herself in the bathroom, and another girl told me to get down. We both squatted on the floor until everything calmed down. The survival skills of these two teenage girls was amazing. They had better skills than me as my initial reaction was to freeze and then run. They reacted instinctively and even helped a teacher in the process. We even had a door behind us for a possible escape just in case whoever was shooting ran into the main office. As we were squatting on the floor, students and staff were still running through the office looking for shelter. Better yet, looking for cover. Coach Clemons ran in and fell to the ground in front of us. He looked at me with panic in his eyes and said, "I've been shot!"

Oh, my god! When he fell to the ground, I could see a bloody circle right above his hip. It got bigger right before my eyes. I told the other student to grab some tissue out of the bathroom, and I stepped across Coach Clemons to grab the phone off the secretary's desk. I pulled it over to where we were, because we still did not know the situation with the shooter. I applied pressure to Coach Clemons' wound and dialed 911. Coach Clemons was in a lot of pain, and I had the female student talk to him to try to keep him calm. Halfway through the description to the 911 dispatcher, someone ran through the office and tripped the phone cord. This could not be happening. I had to remain calm because the student was there and had just showed resiliency. I had to do the same. We got the phone cord back in and completed the call. I think I ended the call prematurely because we had to get more tissue for Coach Clemons. Things begin to settle back down and the school nurse and EMTs had arrived. Our School Resource Officer, Ron Brown, had chased and caught the shooter. The shooter had been a victim of chronic bullying and had his cousin bring a weapon to school. His cousin passed him the gun through the chained doors near the cafeteria and gym. When he saw the group of guys that had been bullying him, he turned and fired up the hall, hoping to hit at least one of them, but he hit Coach Clemons instead. I can remember Mr. Howard complimenting me on my bravery. I can remember my father being outside because the word had gotten out that a history teacher and basketball coach had been shot. Damn. I was a history teacher and a basketball coach.

As Coach Clemons was recovering, Armstrong High School got national attention for all the wrong reasons. As we moved further into the Spring, the players and parents were getting antsy because they didn't want to fall behind in their player development. Especially since we had the potential to be good. Mr. Howard had thought it would be best to delay the announcement that Coach Clemons was no longer the coach while he recuperated. He was right, but it kind of dragged on. Some of it was because Coach

Clemons thought he may get a movie and book deal due to some of the media outlets that had contacted him. I'm not sure if any legal stuff was also going on, but it took months for me to be announced. The players were happy, and the parents were happy, but some of the staff felt that Coach Clemons was not given a chance. I can remember Coach Clemons and Mr. Rakestraw coming to one of our workouts on a Thursday evening and telling me that he felt he had been set up. That Mr. Howard wanted me to have the job the entire time. He explained that it was nothing against me, but he felt that since he won sixteen or seventeen games, that he deserved the job. I did not know what to say. I asked him to be supportive of the kids and hopefully he would feel better and return to teaching. He agreed, but I could tell he was hurt. I felt bad for him but could not let it get in the way of what I was trying to do. I thought we had enough talent to make some noise in the region the following year, and I was going to channel my inner Magic Johnson and put Vernon Hope, the 6'5" small forward at point guard.

I figured that this would be thinking outside the box, but it would also show the players that I knew how to market them. Think about it. This was the late 1990s, and if you were 6'5", you were more than likely to play in the post. It made so much sense to me because Vernon always had the ball in transition anyway because he would get the rebound and just take off dribbling. Because he had a size advantage, I would put two shooters with him on the wings, Greg and Elshod, and have a power-forward who could run and jump too, Gee-Gee who was only 6'3" but could touch the top of the square, and I needed another rebounder at the five. I

This is my first head coaching experience as the Junior-Varsity Head Coach of the Armstrong Mighty Wildcats. Our gear was pretty sweet for a J.V. team!

had a lot of options at that position, so it was a team effort. In Summer League, we were killing teams, averaging 28-29 points a quarter. I can remember Coach Lancaster pointing this out to me when one of the games was in their gym. He said that I may be on to something with Hope. Everything was going to work out so well, all we had to do was make sure Vernon stayed in summer school because he was short one class for eligibility. All he had to do was pass it, but for some strange reason, Vernon just stopped going to summer school. We went by his house. He wasn't there. His team-mates tried to call him, and he wouldn't answer. When we finally got in touch with him, he said that he didn't mean anything by it, but that he just needed a break. A break? When I told him that he wouldn't be able to play because he didn't have the grades, he responded that it didn't matter. He said that he didn't want to play basketball anymore anyway.

We were terrible my first year. We only won five games. I can remember on the Friday before we got out of school for the Christmas break, we had a student versus faculty basketball game. The faculty team was led by myself and one of my assistant coaches, Alga Evans, but it didn't matter. Vernon Hope and Thomas Johnson killed us. Both being 6'5" to 6'6", skilled and athletic. When the game ended, and I was preparing for practice, Vernon walked into the storage area and asked me when I wanted him to report to practice. The report cards had not even come out yet, and he knew that I needed him. I told him I would look at his grades and at Thomas' grades and I would talk to them next week.

When Vernon and Thomas became eligible, we grew tremendously in talent, but the chemistry of the team was thrown off significantly. Vernon believed that he would pick up as the star of the team like it was last summer. The other players wanted to win as well but did not appreciate how he approached the situation, since they had been there all year. Thomas did his best to fit in, and he made an immediate impact when he got into games. Still, it wasn't what I really wanted our team to represent. I was trying to change the culture and provide our players with preparation for life. Because I had the "no cornroll" rule still in effect, Vernon and Thomas decided to just take their cornrolls out and sport the "notty-fro" which is popular today. The "notty fro" of today is really a shorter cut than the seven or eight inches of floppy hair that Thomas and Vernon could barely see through. It looked bad. Mr. Samuels, came to me before the game and asked if I was going to do anything about it. What could I do? They had found a way around my rule that ended up making the team portray a stereotypical image that I was trying to get away from.

In retrospect, I should have just kept playing the guys I had. I allowed the pressure of not winning, people asking if I really knew what I was doing, and just the fact of hating to lose get to me. I compromised my rules with the hope of salvaging a season that was already lost. The next year, I stuck to my guns and laid down the discipline very strongly. We only won six games that year, but we were better at the end of the season than we were at the beginning. I played a lot of younger players in Dante Atkins, Marlon Smith, and Danny Artis. These three guys along with Kendrell Jackson would be our foundation moving forward. However, if we didn't upset Henrico in the Capital District Tournament, I may never have been able to see the fruits of my labor.

We beat Henrico and qualified for the Central Region tournament, and people begin to realize that we might have been building something at Armstrong, if everyone could stay eligible. My third year as head boys' basketball coach, we won nine games but could not beat the elite teams in the area. This was when I decided to study the top programs in greater detail and develop a system to exploit their weaknesses. I had the best opponent to study in Coach Lancaster's programs at Highland Springs. They were a machine, and had been that way since the 1980s. His program would strike fear in several teams just by playing mind games like having his guys warm up at half-time of the varsity girls game or junior varsity boys game and have them put on a show. Shooting threes from twenty-five and thirty

Wildcats win crown in double overtime

Matoaca reigns in Southside

Marlon Smith scored a game-high 34 points, Dwayne Atkins added 29 points, and Armstrong survived a double-overtime duel with Henrico 94-92 to win the Capital District regular-season championship last night.

BOYS

Henrico's Justin Wansley, who scored 21 points, hit a 3-pointer with 9 seconds remaining in regulation, then junior Eric McCray came off the bench and hit a 3 to send the game into double overtime.

The Warriors' luck ran out with 11 seconds remaining in the second OT when Atkins' putback put Armstrong ahead 94-92. Henrico got the ball down the court, then missed two 3-point attemps as time expired.

Eric Claiborne had 19 points and 20 rebounds, and Oliver Holmes scored 15 for the Warriors.

Armstrong...............13 16 20 20 12 13— 94
Henrico.....................20 17 11 21 12 11— 92

Armstrong (10-2 Capital, 15-5) — Baker 1, Atkins 29, Artis 6, K. Jackson 8, S. Jackson 12, M. Smith 34, Jones 2. Totals: 36 20-37 94. 3-point goals: Baker, Atkins.

Henrico (6-6, 12-9) — McCray 8, Grooms 12, Holmes 15, Fells 2, Wansley 21, Hightower 10, Claiborne 19, Trent 0, King 0, Fells 2, Dickerson 3. Totals: 36 16-25 92. 3-point goals: Wansley 2, McCray, Holmes.

JV – Armstrong 58-48.

How the T-D's Boys Top 10 fared

No. Team	Yesterday	Next
1. George Wythe (20-1)	d. Midlothian 73-38	Dominion tourn. (Tues.)
2. Hermitage (19-2)	d. J.R. Tucker 75-57	Colonial tourn. (Tues.)
3. Benedictine (21-3)	did not play	at Roanoke Cath. (today)
4. Highland Springs (15-6)	l. Varina 78-68	Capital tourn. (Tues.)
5. Armstrong (15-5)	d. Henrico 94-92	Capital tourn. (Wed.)
6. Pr. George (17-4)	d. T. Dale 71-65	Central tourn. (Tues.)
7. Thomas Dale (16-5)	l. P. George 71-65	Central tourn. (Tues.)
8. Petersburg (15-5)	d. Col. Heights 63-45	Central tourn. (Tues.)
9. Varina (16-5)	d. H. Springs 78-68	Capital tourn. (Tues.)
10. Hopewell (14-7)	did not play	Central tourn. (Tues.)

I always would love to look in the *Richmond Times-Dispatch* after we won a game. This one was even sweeter because we wrapped up the Capital District Crown!

feet or completing dunk contest-worthy dunks that made the crowd ooh and ah. Pure genius. Before you knew it, they would be up by ten to twelve points in the first quarter because their opponents were still amazed and shocked by what they saw at halftime. Up by ten before the game even starts. That was where I got it from.

I figured if I studied Highland Springs, Franklin McMillan's George Wythe Bulldogs, and Darryl Jenkins'

We did it. I never really thought of anything more than winning the Capital District title. Our league was so competitive and with Armstrong, Highland Springs, Henrico, and Varina, four programs that could beat anybody in the state. We probably could have made some noise in the Regional tournament if Dante wouldn't have turned his ankle in practice two days before the game, and if Marlon wouldn't have rolled his ankle during the game. Again, the bad luck. It also didn't help that the Central District consisting of Prince George, Thomas Dale, Petersburg, and Hopewell were also very good, and we were matched up against each other. Because of some upsets in their district tournament, the seeding changed, and we ended up playing Thomas Dale, even though we had put Petersburg as the opponent on the school marquee. Thomas Dale had Brad Byerson, a 6'9 center that could handle the ball and do it all. The offensive rebounds and stick backs that Dante had come so accustomed to were no longer there due to Brad's size or that he blocked just to send a message. We lost by seven. The greatest season that I had in my young career was now over. It hurt, but again, I used it as motivation. I had already used the speech to my players that no one respected us. I shared how Marlon Smith, who led the district in scoring at 20 points per game, was not voted as a first-team all-district player by one coach, costing him a spot on the first team ballot, and eliminating him from being a player of the year candidate. I don't think this one was bad luck, but more like a coach being irritated that we beat them convincingly, or maybe it was just pure racism. I could not believe how well Marlon Smith handled this unfairness. He was so mature about the situation. He also used it as motivation and he kept things in perspective because he already had a football scholarship to Elizabeth City State University. I honestly think I was madder than he was. I cannot ever remember in my playing days or coaching days an instance of the leading scorer in the district not being on the first team. In the three years prior, the leading scorer in the Capital District was also the player of the year. It still bothers me to this day.

With the season being over, my name began to circulate as a coach that was on the rise. My alma mater, Hermitage High, had just announced that Coach Jenkins was retiring. Oh my. I dreamed of going back to my high school that had so much talent and had great support. I felt that the players would rally around me because ten years prior, I was one of them. The starting point guard for Hermitage, Matt Coward, and I were still close because I knew his mom and his family very well. I can remember he and I talking on the phone about my interest in being his coach and his mom talking to the other parents about who I was. The only issue was that Coach Jenkins, had a top assistant in Joe Coulter, who also wanted the job. Many people believed that he was promised the job. He and I were always cool, but he knew that I had interest, especially when a few of my teammates and I attended Hermitage's sport awards to bid Coach Jenkins a fond farewell. He was so happy to see Jaron, Allee and me. I stayed until the very end when each team had their breakout sessions and Coach Jenkins wanted to thank me for coming. When he finished his remarks and all the awards were distributed, several of the parents approached me in the commons area. They let me know that Mrs. Coward reminded them who I was. They made it clear that they thought it was time for Hermitage to have a black basketball coach. Damn. Here is when I realized that there were politics at every school. Especially for high profile basketball jobs like Hermitage.

A lot of people in the basketball community believed that I was going to be the next coach at Hermitage. I remember when I prepared for my interview, I made sure my portfolio was decked out in Hermitage's colors and improved on my basketball calendar from my original interview at Armstrong. The funny thing is that I wasn't sure if it was the job that I really wanted as much as I did maybe about a month earlier. As all the politicking and political maneuvering was occurring, I received a call from Coach Lancaster. He told me that I needed to take a hard look at Meadowbrook High School. I knew that Meadowbrook had athletes because players like Tyrone Salley was there recently along with Michael Doles, Mark Adams and a few others. Coach Lancaster reminded me that Mike Moreau had just left the program about a year ago and that the junior varsity coach had taken over. I was so wrapped up in my own team and keeping an eye on Hermitage that I had completely forgotten about it. Coach Lancaster was very close with the Principal at Meadowbrook, Joe Oley, who called him about hiring a new coach. Coach Lancaster told him that I was the guy to hire. Coach Lancaster let Mr. Oley know that I was looking to leave Armstrong because I needed "a better facility." Those were his words not mine. I got a call from Mr. Oley the same night and he asked me to come by the school after work so that we could sit down and talk. I informed Mr. Oley that I had an end of the day planning period and could be there around 2:00 or so. I let Mr. Hopkins know of my intentions and signed out. When I arrived at Meadowbrook, there was construction equipment and vehicles everywhere. No one told me that the school was in the middle of a renovation. As I entered through the dust and clouds of smoke, the main office was already finished. I waited in a lobby that looked so much newer and larger than the one we had at Armstrong. Mr. Oley came down the hall to meet me and gave me a hug. Wow. I really wasn't expecting that. He sat me down in his office and let me know that they had targeted me in their efforts to hire a new basketball coach. He told me that Meadowbrook was a basketball school and even though the football team was improving, it was still going to be a basketball school.

He began to walk me around the building showing me the new parts of the building versus the older, more narrow parts of the building. When he took me into the auxiliary gym, it hit me that this was the same gym that Michael Torrence, Michael Petin, Kevin Connor, and I had worked out in over the summer in the 1990s. It was a nice gym then, but now was considered the auxiliary gym. Mr. Oley could see me looking at the old scoreboard and bleachers and being a little bit puzzled. He told me that I could use this gym for JV practices or walkthroughs when the real game was going on in the new gym. I could not wait to see it. He took me down the steps into a gymnasium lobby that had vaulted ceilings and trophy cases. I could see bright lights and parquet floors through the door windows. I could not wait to go in.

When we entered the gymnasium, the first thing that I noticed was that there were three full courts, six baskets, plenty of space, and bleachers that were big enough to hold two thousand people. I didn't even notice the four or five PE classes that were in the gym. I was so amazed at the size of the facility that nothing else even mattered. Mr. Oley walked me through the gym and pointed out the baskets, the brand new floor, the storage areas, and said that we were going to meet Mr. Higginbotham, the athletic director. As we entered the back hall, Mr. Oley paused to show me the basketball locker rooms. College size lockers, with their own whiteboard, entryway to the bathrooms and showers, and benches for the kids to sit on in front of their lockers. It was like I walked into a Division I basketball program at the high school level.

I tried so hard to contain how excited I was so that Mr. Oley would not notice. When we came out of the locker room, Mr. Higginbotham was waiting for us in the hallway. He showed me the weight room, which had four benches, two squat racks, and every set of dumbbells from 10 to 100 pounds. I was so excited about the amount of space and began to envision my teams working out to get bigger, stronger, and faster. Mr. Higginbotham and Mr. Oley then took me into Mr. Higginbotham's office and talked to me about building a program. They told me that they thought very highly of Coach Lancaster, and when he recommended me, that was all they needed. They reminded me of how impressed they were with my coaching style and how I handled my team in our victory over Meadowbrook that season. By this time the physical education classes were ending, and they walked me back into the gymnasium one more time before they took me back to Mr. Oley's office. As I entered, Mr. Higginbotham turned on the Chicago Bulls, intro music that rang through about twenty speakers. They timed it perfectly. I felt like Jordan as I was walking up the sideline. I am sure that Mr. Oley noticed the smile on my face, because he leaned over and said, "This could all be yours in a couple of months." I was sold.

The interview for the Hermitage job rent well. Mr. Bruce Bowen, my athletic director when I was a student there was still in the same position, and he commented to me several times during the interview how impressed he was with me. When Mr. Blackburn, the principal, asked me a question about how I would monitor my player's grades, Mr. Bowen answered the question for me and said, "It's in there" like the Ragu spaghetti sauce commercials. They took me out the back door an hour later and said that they would be in touch in a few weeks.

During that time frame, my new athletic director Bob Gary, informed me that he had put in a few kind words with Bruce Bowen about my interest in the Hermitage basketball position. I am still not sure how he found out I was interested, because I never told him. I guess it wasn't that big of a secret, but he had no idea that I also had interviewed at Meadowbrook. In that interview, I felt no pressure because of my prior visit. I switched up a lot of things from my Hermitage portfolio and described my goal of making Meadowbrook a National Basketball program. I can remember Mr. Ted Reynolds, who was an assistant principal at the time, telling me that I should have been a marketing teacher instead of a history teacher because I could sell anything. Meadowbrook offered me the job about a week later, but I still had not heard back from Hermitage. I put in a phone call to Patrice Pruden, who was one of the leaders in Human Resources, to inform her that I was going to withdraw my name and take the job at Meadowbrook High School. I think she must have read my mind, because she let me know that another candidate had been chosen for the Hermitage job, but that they hadn't gotten around to inform the other candidates yet. It is funny how things kind of work out for you when you are patient.

As soon as I got to Meadowbrook, I automatically assumed that the experience was going to be very similar to my high school experience at Hermitage High School. I had heard the stories about how the demographics had changed and how Meadowbrook was more "black" now, but all I knew was that most of these kids were in better situations at home than many of the kids at Armstrong. I did wonder, however, if my players were going to be as tough and resilient as my players at Armstrong. That was something that concerned me. I always knew how to motivate Dante, Marlon, Shawn Jackson, and L. C. Baker. I knew that even if we were down late in a game, they were not going to give up. I had a chance to have a sneak peek into the talent at Meadowbrook, as we'd played them in my last season at Armstrong. Meadowbrook had athletes, and lots of them, but they did not seem to play hard all the time. It also seemed that they were a little selfish and seemed to care more about their own personal stats instead of the actual score on the scoreboard. When I met with the players during an open gym, I was amazed at the turnout. We had like ninety players show up for open gym. I guess I had to remember that I wasn't at a school that had 535 students anymore, and that the talent pool was going to be larger. Now don't get me wrong, out of those ninety, only about the junior varsity and ninth grade players were playing. I then caught a glance of a 6'3" freshman who looked like Lebron James playing with people his age. He truly was a man among boys. He drove baseline and dunked on like two guys. It took me a second to remember that when I had my informational meeting the week before, I asked Michael Jefferson to show me who was this freshman who went by "DJ." When I met Devin Johnson, he was kind of shy, but I could tell he was serious about basketball. A few months later during tryouts, as the players were walking into the locker room, Devin was about to sit with the junior varsity prospects. I pulled him aside and said that he was coming with us. He looked at me with both excitement and nervousness. I told him that he was going to be my starting point guard for the next four years, and that this was going to be the beginning of something that would last for a lifetime.

As I already have informed all of you that are reading this great, inspirational journey, if you don't have good guards, you don't win. The only reason I turned my coaching career around at Armstrong was because I was lucky enough to have L. C. Baker enroll at Franklin Military School, which was housed in Armstrong's building. L. C. was only 5'5" at the time, but he had to be the fastest player I had ever coached, and the best part was that he made great decisions. As he got older, a little stronger, and developed his outside shot, he quickly turned into an All Capital-District Player. Our fast break took on a new level, and more importantly, seniors such as K. D. Jackson, Danny Artis, Dante Atkins, and Marlon Smith respected his game. Leaving him at Armstrong was probably one of the toughest conversations that I had on the phone. What was shocking was that L. C. was happy for me and hoped that one of my assistants would get the job so that he could play for a coach that he knows and respects. So, in DJ, I saw an opportunity to mold a freshman from day one, and he was so physically gifted, I knew that the sky was going to be the limit for this kid.

Our practices in Year One at Meadowbrook were legendary. Five on five scrimmages and our infamous "shell drill" provided great levels of competition, brotherhood, and a true desire to get better as basketball players. I also liked the fact that all my players had good grades. I did not think I was going to have to worry about a Vernon Hope situation with any of them, as the majority had grade point averages of about a 3.0, and the others were close to it. It still baffled me that this group of talent had only won nine games the previous year. My players thought I was cool, and they respected the fact that my assistants and I would play with them in open gym and lift weights with them during our workouts.

I always believed that creating a staff of people who I could trust and who were friends made my job easier. So, besides bringing along Coach Brown, who I had known since the ninth grade, I also brought in Coach Jamal Miles, who has been one of my closest friends since I was four, and Coach Percy Brewer I had known since middle school. I also decided to bring in one of my former teammates in Coach Jaron Dandridge, who played at Hermitage with me, and helped to create one of the best three-on-three teams in Virginia during our playing days. My players loved the fact that I had a bunch of "able-bodied" coaches around that could get out there and show them some things and help keep things competitive. I knew how they felt because we always seemed to have a little more of an edge to us when I was a student at Hermitage and Coach Roger Jones would play with us. Coach Jones always picked his own teams and made sure I was against him so that he could guard me. We usually let the players pick their teams, and sometimes it was a shock when they would pick some of the coaches with the first or second pick. We had a lot of fun that year and increased the win total to fifteen games. We finished second in the district, qualified for the regional tournament, and helped Michael Jefferson, Tim Berkley, Kenny Webster, and Aaron Wilson earn full basketball scholarships. Our program was getting off to a great start.

Year two of the program brought about great expectations. We felt that with the players that were returning, mainly Devin Johnson, Tony Archie, and Linwood Hurdle, and the strong talent that was moving up from the junior varsity under Coach Brown, that we were setting ourselves up to be good for the next couple of years. I mean really good. Junior varsity players such as Brandon Macklin, T. J. Peterkin, A. J. Pace, and Roy Haliburton would help us create some depth at each position. We also had Dontrell Jones (who was Jarrell's little brother and coming off a knee injury) ready to play. Realistically, we knew we were young in varsity experience, but we also knew that besides maybe L. C. Bird, who had Tyreese Rice—a future all-state performer—we could beat anybody. I can remember DJ calling me one night and letting me know that his friend Marty Harrison wanted to transfer schools and enroll at Meadowbrook. I knew who Marty was due to some of our games vs. Monacan High School. Marty was a real cerebral player who was about 6'2" and very strong. He wasn't the best season, Devin hurt his knee in a freak collision and was out for four to six weeks. When we played against Benedictine in a tournament later in the year, Brandon decides to challenge Bombale Osby on a dunk-attempt. Osby was about 6'7" and 230 pounds of pure muscle; when he blocked the dunk attempt, Brandon fell awkwardly, and his leg got caught underneath of him. I thought he had broken his leg, but it ended up being a really bad sprain of several ligaments. He only missed a few games, but he was never the same for the rest of the season. The team had other players that stepped up in the absence of those two guys. Marty Harrison moved into the starting line-up in DJ's place. Linwood Hurdle became a lot more aggressive at the offensive end and ended up shooting almost 60 percent from the three-point line. It is still a shock when I think about this guy almost hitting 60 percent from the three. Tony Archie and Dontrell Jones took advantage of their minutes increasing and became go-to guys at times during the season. Ole did a solid job of filling in for Brandon and we made due. By the end of the season, Devin had returned from injury and showed no-signs of being hesitant or fearful of his knee. We won 17 games, almost made it to the final four of the region and officially announced ourselves as the next basketball power in the Central Region of Virginia.

When I was hired as the new basketball coach at Meadowbrook, I remember telling Mr. Oley and Mr. Higginbotham that we would have championships by our third year in the program. I figured it would take a couple of years to fully have the team buying into our philosophy but also understanding that the Meadowbrook Men's Basketball Program was a culture. As I said in one of our end of the season highlight videos, our players would be "GQ" on game days and "silky-smooth" on the court. During my tenure we began to have basketball camps in the summer months and required all our players to attend. Shawn Barber, one of my closest friends, had just earned a new football contract with the Kansas City Chiefs, and let me know that he would take care of our programs' basketball shoes as long as he was playing. Every year he would send me a check for $3,000 to buy thirty pairs of shoes. Because Devin's reputation as one of the best basketball players in the nation was now growing, I began to get shoe offers from Reebok and Nike. It was everything that I dreamed about and believed that we could do. In my last year at Armstrong, I started this tradition of having a basketball poster that featured our players and our schedule. Just like the colleges. It is interesting to see how a lot of the programs in the Richmond area now do the same, and many of the current coaches credit me for giving them the idea. Those posters at both Meadowbrook and Armstrong were some of the hottest items, if you could get your hands on them. Mrs. Delphine Crump, who was a friend of Shavonne's, was our photographer, and did an outstanding job of taking my ideas of how I wanted the poster to look and turning it into memories that would last a lifetime.

Year Three was here. We knew we were going to be good. We knew that this was the year that we circled that we would start winning championships. Because we were the Meadowbrook Monarchs, I decided to do something a little different with our poster. At Armstrong, we had all the players wear their uniforms and we would gather at half-court or up against a wall for the poster. At Meadowbrook, we took the poster picture in Year one with the school mascot, and under the front archway of the school with the letters Meadowbrook High School in the background. For this year, I decided to show another side of the players and we took the picture before one of our away games. I told all the guys to wear your best "GQ" outfit as tomorrow was poster day. They were so excited. I asked our athletic director to change the lettering on the school marquee to say, "The Monarchy Begins." All the players gathered around the marquee, and I had A. J. Roy, and Chris sit on top of the sign mainly because they were the three shortest guys. As usual, the captains held the basketballs, but I decided that this poster would not include the coaches. It was all about the players. This poster was so hot, and in such high demand, that I had to place three or four orders. Delphine even paid for some of the posters out of her own pocket. Such a sweet lady, and may she rest in peace. I loved it when we would always receive compliments on how good the guys looked in the poster, and how everyone liked that the players not only dressed up on away games, but that they took it to another level and wore suits. I mean I already had the rule, and hopefully modeled it well, that all the coaches would wear suits on the sideline. It made me so proud when we would enter the gym and the people would say "Those must be the players from Meadowbrook. They all dress so well." That was almost as good as saying that we were the best team in the area. And we had a strong following that believed that as well.

Coach Miles, who oversaw our perimeter players, and I had several discussions on who would be our starting lineup this year. We had a lot of guards and very few big men. I knew that Devin and AJ would start, along with Brandon and TJ in the post. But we originally could not settle on the fifth starter. Coach Miles let me know that we should start three guards in Devin, AJ, and Marty. He brought up good points in that Devin, who had grown about an inch or inch and a half, was big enough to play the small forward defensively, but was still able to be effective on offense. I was such a traditionalist in thinking that I always needed to have two guards, two forwards, and a center, that it took me a little while to see that the line-up Coach Miles suggested was our best line-up. The thought that now I could have three players that could initiate the offense was exciting, and with the insertion of Marty into the line-up it would allow Devin and AJ to play off the ball even more. Marty really was a true point guard, AJ was more of a scorer as well as our best shooter, and Devin was our best slasher. It made so much sense. With players like Roy Haliburton, Dontrell Jones, Barry French, and Shawn Outen coming off the bench, we were legitimately nine deep. In a lot of the games, the outcome was decided by half-time. AJ, DJ, and Marty were beating people off the dribble all the time, and because of AJ's great defensive pressure, and the fact that the guys had now been running the same system for three years, they executed at a high level. We won the North-South Tournament to open the season. Even though Hanover High School, had Ed Davis, who still plays in the NBA, we still beat them by twenty. We won the Richmond-Times Dispatch tournament, ironically over Hermitage High School, due to two clutch free throws at the end of the game by Dontrell Jones. We capped it off by winning the very tough Central District by at least three games in the standings. We were good, and now set our sights on the Regional Championship.

We breezed through the first two games of the Regional tournament, and faced off against Henrico in one semi-final, while L. C. Bird and Tyreese Rice, faced off against Highland Springs in the other. These four teams were the best four teams all season. L. C. Bird edged Highland Springs in the first semi-final as I can remember a questionable no-call that went against Highland Springs at the end of the game. They lost by two. Everyone thought that there was going to be a rematch of the epic rival match-up of L. C. Bird vs. Meadowbrook in the final. Henrico had other plans. Coach Vance Harmon, who has won several state championships in the last couple of years, had developed a team that quietly was just as athletic as we were. I remember on the first play of the game, one of the Henrico players shot a jumpshot from in front of our bench. As I am yelling out "rebound" or "box-out" Justin Wansley comes from the left wing and does a one-handed follow-up dunk over our big guys. My players kind of looked at each other and were in shock. Throughout the game, Henrico outworked us and kept getting offensive rebound after offensive rebound. We finally battled back and cut the lead to one late in the game. As Devin drives to the rim, he stepped on someone's foot and turned his ankle. I couldn't believe this was happening. He comes out for a little while but begged me to go back into the game. I was thinking that this was my best player, and maybe he wasn't as hurt as I thought. While he was out, AJ took over the game for us, and we started to run plays for him.

With ten seconds left on the clock, AJ got an outlet pass and made a move to the basket in transition. He pulled up from about six feet and gets fouled, but there was no whistle. I am arguing with the ref that he was not going to shoot an airball from six feet. Henrico got the rebound, and of course we had to foul. They made both free throws and were now up by three, but we have time to advance the ball to half-court and call timeout. I wanted Devin to take the ball out, but he yelled at me "no," as he wanted to have an opportunity to take the last shot. Marty took it out, and I thought he was going to pass the ball to TJ who could shoot the three very well for a big man and was open. Instead, Marty passes it to DJ who rushes and shoots a one-legged floater that ended up being an airball. I couldn't believe we lost that way. And it hurt.

The only good thing about losing vs. Henrico in year three is that it really motivated us in year four. Year four at Meadowbrook High School was going to be special because we had the same set of players that had been running our system for four years. Our starting line-up was already determined because of the experience and leadership that we had from our seniors. At guard would be Marty and D. J. Dontrell would move into the starting line-up at the small forward position and he would be joined at the power-forward by Shawn Outen. By this time, Shawn had become a "beast" in the weight room and had become so strong. I couldn't believe how he had put on ten to fifteen pounds of muscle in only a couple of months. B-Mac, also returned at the center spot and expanded his game to be more than a roll player. We could run plays for him, he could handle the ball, and for some reason, he showed me that he was a consistent three-point shooter from the corners. Off the bench, we had Justin Harper, who was now approaching 6-8 but had the prettiest jump shot on the team. We always believed in allowing players to play to their strengths, and even though most people thought he was a center, he was really a very tall small-forward. Complementing Justin was P. J. Finn, a sophomore who was a rebounding machine, and Ahmad Bizzell, who we hoped would re-create some of the speed that we lost when AJ graduated. We knew we had eight solid players, and when you have great teammates like Norvell Cooper and Darius Green, we had the perfect combination of athleticism, basketball knowledge, strength, and experience. The theme for year for was "The Saga Continues."

By this time everyone knew who Meadowbrook Basketball was. The players were signing autographs. I took the starting five to Five-Star Basketball Camp over the summer to help get them a little more exposure, and all it did was help our national profile. Meadowbrook Men's Basketball was now a "National Program" instead of just being one of the better programs in the state. We once again won the North-South Championship, we were the first team to ever repeat as champions of the Richmond Times-Dispatch Holiday Tournament. We were the first Meadowbrook team to win the Central District Championship back to back. The players had fans and so many colleges recruiting them for their services. We won twenty-four games that year and advanced to the Regional Semi-final game to play L. C. Bird. We had already beaten Bird earlier in the season convincingly at their place and ended the game on a perfectly designed play (if I say so myself) that allowed Devin to do a self alley-oop dunk worthy of any dunk contest. L. C. Bird always had great talent, but this year, they couldn't shoot as well as they had in the past. I had to remember that those kids had been through a lot since their coach, Randy Cave, had passed away earlier in the year. Those are some tough times to go through. For some reason, in this Regional semi-final game, Bird came out on fire. I mean they made like five of their first six three-point attempts, and we couldn't make anything. As the game goes, back and forth, I begin to think that this very successful season was not going to end the way I wanted it. I called a time-out with 1:53 left on the clock, and we were down by ten. I was about to go into my finish strong speech when Devin looked at us and the team and said, "I love you muthaf***as."

We all just paused.

He then smiled and said, "We aren't going to lose this game."

He took over. He scored on our next possession, got a rebound, and took it coast to coast and scored again. Bird turned the ball over, and he found Shawn Outen wide open for a lay-up and a foul. Shawn made the free throw and we are now down three. Bird missed their free throws, and Marty created an easy bucket in the lane and we were now down one. All of this happened in like fifty-five seconds. We fouled again, and Bird made one of two free throws. Dontrell scored at the other end, and now the game was tied. With fifteen seconds left on the clock, Bird had the ball and we had to foul again. We picked one of their worst free throw shooters to foul and he made one of two. We are down one, and Martin Harrison found a way to create again and he gets fouled. He made both of his free throws and now we are up one with eight seconds to go. Bird comes down and misses a wide-open jump shot. They get the rebound, Brandon tries to block the shot, misses, and they get it again, as their player is going up for the put-back, the horn sounds, and the referee puts his hand in the air to signal the foul. He then waves off the foul and gives the signal that the game was over. We were off to the Central Region Championship game and an automatic birth in the State Tournament. I put my arms in the air like we had just won the heavyweight championship of the world. I couldn't believe that we had come back to win that game. All because Devin Johnson said, we were not going to lose.

In the region championship, we had to play perennial power Highland Springs HS. We had already defeated Highland Springs early in the season in the championship game of the Richmond Times-Dispatch tournament, but I knew that Coach Lancaster was going to have some special things up his sleeve for this one. Luckily for me, Devin gave one of the best pre-game speeches that I have ever heard. He talked to the players about being a family, how as seniors, winning this game would solidify their legacy in Meadowbrook History, and how we could not let each other down. All I could do was sit back and listen in awe as there was no longer a need for my pregame speech. You know when you are doing a great job as a coach when the players say what you are going to say before you do. I have never been prouder of my players. They played a great game. Highland Springs is always so good that you can never dominate them, but we never trailed and won by ten. Meadowbrook High School had never won the Central Region Championship in boys' basketball. We made history, just like Devin said we would.

Chapter 5

Reflections:

1) As an educator, how do you find ways to motivate your students? Do you think it is more extrinsic or intrinsic motivation?

2) What do you think are the steps necessary to build a solid team? What should you do first? How do you know if your team is being successful? (This does not just relate to athletics, but could be a team of leaders, teachers, etc.)

3) In education today, many leaders are asked to be coaches and mentors. What strategies do you use to coach someone to improve? How do you differ between being a coach and being a mentor?

4) It has been said that coaches many times judge their success by how many of their assistants or former players become coaches themselves. Think of the Bill Walsh coaching tree. What would be some of the first advice that you would give a new coach or a new leader? How can you help them be successful even though it is not your team, program, school, etc.?

These three teams represent the legacy of Coach Gordon. Besides all of the championships that we won together, the brotherhood that was established is still strong to this day. Thank you fellas!

Meadowbrook Men's Basketball
2004 - 2005

Thursday	12/02/04	Lee Davis @ L. D.	7:30p	Tuesday	01/11/05	Matoaca	7:30p(H)
Friday	12/03/04	North/South @ Lee Davis	TBA	Friday	01/14/05	Prince George High	7:30p
Saturday	12/04/04	North/South @ Hanover	TBA	Saturday	01/15/05	Bird High School	7:30p(H)
Tuesday	12/07/04	Hopewell High	7:70p(H)	Tuesday	01/18/05	Thomas Dale High	7:30p(H)
Friday	12/10/04	Thomas Dalye High	7:30p	Friday	01/21/05	Dinwiddie High	7:30p
Tuesday	12/14/04	Dinwiddie High	7:30p(H)	Friday	01/28/05	Hopewell High	7:30p
Thursday	12/16/04	In Sync	TBA	Tuesday	02/01/05	Colonial Heights High	7:30p
Friday	12/17/04	In Sync	TBA	Friday	02/04/05	Petersburg High	7:30p(H)
Saturday	12/18/04	In Sync	TBA	Tuesday	02/08/05	Matoaca	7:30p
Monday	12/20/04	In Sync	TBA	Friday	02/11/05	Prince George High	7:30p(H)
Tuesday	01/04/05	Colonial Heights High	7:30p(H)	Tuesday	02/15/05	District Tournament	TBA
Friday	01/07/05	Petersburg High	7:30p	Thursday	02/17/05	Dist. Tourn. @ T. D.	TBA

The Saga Continues . . .

Meadowbrook Men's Basketball
2005-2006
Schedule

Thursday	12/1/05	Monacan High	7:30 pm
Tuesday	12/6/05	Thomas Dale High	7:30 pm
Friday	12/9/05	Dinwiddie High	7:30 pm (H)
Saturday	12/10/05	Maury	5:00 pm (H)
Tuesday	12/13/05	Matoaca	7:30 pm
Friday	12/16/05	Times Dispatch Tournament	TBA
Saturday	12/17/05	Times Dispatch Tournament	TBA
Monday	12/19/05	Times Dispatch Tournament	TBA
Tuesday	12/20/05	Times Dispatch Tournament	TBA
Tuesday	01/03/06	Petersburg High	7:30 pm
Friday	01/06/06	Prince George High	7:30 pm (H)
Monday	01/09/06	George Wythe High	7:30 pm (H)
Tuesday	01/10/06	Hopewell High	7:30 pm (H)
Friday	01/13/06	Colonial Heights High	7:30 pm
Tuesday	01/17/06	Matoaca	7:30 pm (H)
Thursday	01/19/06	Thomas Dale High	7:30 pm (H)
Friday	01/20/06	Slam Fest	TBA
Friday	01/27/06	Dinwiddie High	7:30 pm
Monday	01/30/06	Lloyd C. Bird High	7:30 pm
Tuesday	01/31/06	Petersburg High	7:30 pm (H)
Friday	02/03/06	Prince George High	7:30 pm
Tuesday	02/07/06	Hopewell High	7:30 pm
Friday	02/10/06	Colonial Heights High	7:30 pm (H)
Tuesday	02/14/06	District Tournament at Higher Seed	TBA
Thursday	02/16/06	District Tournament at Hopewell	TBA
Friday	02/17/06	District Tournament at Hopewell	TBA

Chapter 6

The Administrator

If you took a poll of people in education today, an overwhelming percentage would probably say that being a teacher is the hardest part of being an educator. I think I would slightly disagree. Being an administrator is extremely difficult due to the need to manage students, parents, and the faculty. You are becoming a teacher of all three. Instead of only affecting the hundred-plus students you teach, the number multiplies in administration. You now must assist in the education of the student, the teacher, his/her parents, their uncles, the grandparents who are on the pick-up list, and the older brother that you almost expelled from school when he was here. He doesn't like you. It was told to me by a certain director of human resources that the teachers that they want to become administrators should be the "best of the best." Every time I hear that phrase, I always think of the terrible karate movie from the 80s that I can't help but watch every time it comes on. Being best of the best means that you are well-respected, you do more at school than just teach, and you are trusted by your current administration. Oh, and don't forget having really good test scores, low discipline, and the ability to get along with everyone no matter their quirks. I was very hesitant to go into administration due to my love of coaching basketball and seeing how much stress administrators were under every time I would talk to them. They seemed to "gray" right in front of my eyes and always had to rush off to handle something of the utmost importance. The first administrator that I worked with at East Salisbury Elementary School on the eastern shore of Maryland, was never happy. I don't think I can ever remember her smiling about anything. The year before I got there, I was told that she was formerly in Central Office and was moved to the building to help clean it up. Some said she was moved there to punish her. East Salisbury Elementary School was in one of the poorer areas of the county, and the students had more serious things to worry about than passing the ever so important MSPAP State Assessment. These students had to worry about survival due to constant gunfire, drugs, the inability to pay rent, and parents who really did not care. Think about a ten-year old student with that many obstacles to overcome before they get to middle school. The goal of our administrators at East Salisbury was to increase MSPAP scores, increase parent involvement, and to keep the ship afloat in so many words.

In seeing this for the first time, I had no idea that my first job was going to be like this. I was the typical "ready to save the world" guy because I always had a great relationship with kids. As a fifth grade teacher, who grew up in the suburbs of Henrico County, I always thought that all fifth graders wanted to learn. Would do what the teacher would ask of them or fear the wrath that they would receive from examples of posting my classroom rules, how they should be written, and where I should put them. Even though I had zero teaching experience, I thought that some of my ideas were very good, and I disagreed with some of her suggestions. She reported me to the principal. The principal, who I had only talked with once or twice, sent the AP to come and talk to me. Maybe she did it because we both were black and thought she could get through to me more. When the assistant principal met with me, she went over the suggestions from the new teacher advisor and wrote down my ideas. She then came up with a compromise between the two that satisfied both the county mandates, without stifling my creativity. This was my first look into how a good administrator works, and how effective communication and collaboration can be. For compromise, she took input from both sources and dissolved the communication barrier by becoming my chief point of contact. This was a great example of an administrator fixing a problem and keeping everyone at the table happy. I didn't stay at East Salisbury Elementary School past that year because I wanted to return to the Richmond area. Because my mother was currently an administrator at Richmond Public Schools (RPS), I knew I had a shot at getting a job there. My mom used her contacts in City Hall to get me two interviews.

Now I had heard all the horror stories about Richmond Public Schools due to my mother working there almost her entire career. I thought that I would be able to make a difference and relate to the students because of my age, interest in sports, and the fact that my grandfather was the preacher at one of the more predominant churches in the city. What I did not count on was the disorganization of

RPS at the time. My first interview was with Mr. Carlton Stevens, who was the principal of Huguenot High School. I was excited about this opportunity because Mr. Stevens was one of my dad's closest friends, his son and I played basketball together and was one of my role models growing up, and they also had a basketball coaching opening. The crazy part is that the human resources department sent me on this interview after the teaching vacancy had already been filled. I still don't understand that to this day. When I met with Mr. Stevens, he said that this was like interviewing his son, and that he had hoped he could bring me along and make me a part of the Falcon family. He apologized for the mix-up and offered to help me in any way he could. He got on the phone and called Gerry Howard, Principal at Armstrong High School, to see if he still had an opening. He did, and I was off to interview at Armstrong the next day. Mr. Stevens was very professional and a handsome guy who exuded confidence. He did remind me of my father, but it was different seeing him in his professional role, instead of just being the men's fellowship leader at church. It was at this time that I saw how being an administrator is a role that is well respected in your community, and paints the picture of being caring, knowledgeable, and connected. The fact that Mr. Howard and Mr. Stevens had a good relationship, allowed me to move closer to becoming a teacher. Mr. Stevens' phone call superseded the phone call from the Human Resources Department from RPS.

During my interview with Mr. Howard I noticed that he was an older gentleman who had been with RPS his entire career. He knew my mother very well and was an excellent golfer. He also had a great way of seeing through any "BS" that would come his way from his school community. At Armstrong High School - the school in which my entire family on both sides attended there was a sense of pride, elitism, and unfortunately those who wanted something for free. Even though Mr. Howard had been well known in the area, the kids didn't respect him. They always would make up stories about how he was on drugs, sold drugs, or something because he always had wads of money in his pocket. That was the issue. Even if he believed in carrying that much cash, why are you showing it to people? How did the kids know? This perception of Mr. Howard gave me one of my first lessons of perception being reality. We had two things that happened at Armstrong that would forever change the way I viewed the administration. The first was the Virginia Standards of Learning (SOL) began my first year as a teacher. This new test was going to change how students and schools were to be viewed using an end of the year multiple choice assessment. The first year when the scores came back, there was outrage across the Commonwealth of Virginia. Not one school division did well. Passing rates were in the twenties, and wealthy parents complained that the test was too hard. When Armstrong had a passing rate of 14 percent, it was no surprise. Instead of discussing with parents how he would improve the scores, Mr. Howard focused on how all the "white" schools in the area did poorly too. Armstrong High School was just like everyone else, so don't worry. I couldn't believe it. The parents bought it. Hook, line, and sinker. At the end of his speech as Mr. Howard strutted out of the classroom, he turns to me and another teacher, straightens out his jacket and says, "winging it!" And he did.

Mr. Howard also knew his community. He was a salesman who could talk his way out of almost anything. Mr. Howard did not back down from the threats, even though we had neighborhood fights that would cause the entire school to go on lockdown. Mr. Howard would then walk through the halls and have security grab the perpetrators so that everyone could see. During basketball games, he would pull up his chair to the half-court line on the opposite side of the gym and just watch the coach. Very intimidating. He wouldn't watch the game, but he would watch the actions of the cheerleaders, the fans, and if someone was trying to sneak in. From him I learned the importance of making your presence known. Everyone knew who Mr. Howard was. He made himself very visible when he would enter an area of his school. If he came to observe you, he would eventually take over the class and teach the lesson for you. This was his way of showing the students that because he is a good teacher, he can teach any subject, and at any time. The teachers hated it when he did that. It made them feel that he did not respect their position, or their time since they were preparing for the Virginia SOL's. Some teachers used to call him on it. A mistake. You then were placed on Howard's list and you would be gone soon. If you happened to stay, your teaching life would suddenly become a lot harder than it should in a school with three housing projects. That did not matter to Mr. Howard because you weren't loyal to the direction of the school. He felt that you were putting your individual beliefs ahead of the school beliefs. That is why he referred to the school as the Armstrong Mighty Wildcats. Not Armstrong Wildcats. Armstrong Mighty Wildcats. (Just imagine Mr. Howard saying this in friend from the neighborhood, made his way outside to let him know that I was ok.

Mr. Howard did it again. He took this tragedy -teacher getting shot, a student who just ruined his life and would probably spend a lot of time in jail, and the fact that our school is now confirmed unsafe- and turned it into great publicity. He worked with Governor Gilmore to sign Virginia's version of a safe schools act, with Armstrong High School as the backdrop. As Mr. Howard summoned me to his office, he introduced me as the first-year teacher who made the 911 call and acted like a ten-year veteran. He wanted me to be close on the press footage and maybe get me in a photoshoot at the governor's live press conference. He could sell the school. Mr. Howard could have been a believer in the tale that all publicity is good publicity. It didn't end well as the next year, he was removed as principal due to financial inaccuracies.

The day that Mr. Howard was removed from being principal, I can remember April Hawkins, who ironically became a principal at Armstrong High School, coming into my classroom and going to my desk to write vigorously. As I am teaching my lesson on Geography, I am wondering what she is writing and giving me this funny look. As the bell rings to end class, April hands me a note that says that Mr. Howard, Ms. Leonard (the School Accountant) and one of the secretaries had all been fired! I literally looked at her and mouthed "What the hell?" She whispered that the money wasn't right and that there was improper spending and record-keeping. After I got over my initial shock, I went downstairs and saw the superintendent of schools, Dr. Williams, and three or four other people from City

Hall in suits in the main office and the front hallway. The superintendent already had a reputation for being really hard and wanting to clean up Richmond City Schools. He looked at me, didn't say anything, and then he ushered the two assistant principals into Mr. Howard's office. I did not want to stick around to see what happened, but of course there was a faculty meeting at the end of the day. At this meeting the two assistant principals explained to us that Mr. Howard had been placed on administrative leave and that they were not sure when or if he was coming back. The meeting was kind of sad, except for the teachers who were on Howard's "hit list" and stated he had it coming and they were excited to see who the new principal would be. Now it was obvious to all of us that neither one of our current assistant principals were going to become the new principal because neither of them had enough presence to be able to run the school effectively. Especially with everything that went down.

At our next faculty meeting a few weeks later, Dr. Williams, RPS Superintendent, was present. We all knew that we were going to find out Mr. Howard's fate at this meeting. Dr. Williams announced that Mr. Howard had "retired" and that he hired an interim principal to close out the year until they could find the right person for the job. He introduced us to Mr. Joe Louis Simmons, a tall thin older gentleman who seemed to not have a hair out of place. As soon as the meeting was over, I asked some of the veteran teachers what they knew about Mr. Simmons. They spoke of him like a god. He was a retired principal that cleaned up every school that he led. He met with every teacher over the next couple of weeks to introduce himself and to discuss the transition. When he met with me, he told me that he knew my entire family and that he heard what I'd done during the shooting. He also knew that I was the basketball coach, but more importantly a leader in the school. I am thinking, who gave him this information? What did I do at twenty-four years old that gave me the moniker of being a leader? He then let me know that he was going to be counting on me to help keep our athletic programs be successful because our kids and the community needed something to cheer about. From Mr. Simmons, I learned the aspect of being a personable administrator. The demeanor that he possessed in faculty meetings and the way that he communicated with people was second to none. Even when he was reprimanding someone, he did it in a very respectful way, and it almost got to the point that you did not want to disappoint him. As the school year ended he made it very clear that he was not returning the following year. This caused a sense of uneasiness because both the faculty and the students adapted well to Mr. Simmons' leadership style. Some of the faculty had more of the attitude of here we go again with a new principal in the building. We soon got the word that Mr. Howard Hopkins, principal at one of our feeder middle schools would become our new principal.

Mr. Hopkins, fondly known as "Hop" to all people in Richmond Public Schools that knew him, was a shorter guy who was in his early fifties when he took the job. I heard that he was a bundle of energy, took no mess, and was known as a change agent. I also heard that he was a former athletic director, basketball coach, and all-around leader that wanted everything done right. I was a little nervous to meet him because I heard that he was not happy with the current win/loss totals of the boys' basketball team. If you remember, during my first year as coach, I went 5–16. The team was awful, but I had a bunch of young guys playing, and now they had a year of experience under their belt. The rumor mill had it be known that Mr. Hopkins was going to bring his middle school basketball coach to Armstrong with him, and place him on my staff, and eventually replace me with him as head coach. I couldn't have that. I went to see Mr. Hopkins at his middle school faculty meeting in which he announced he was leaving and going to Armstrong High School. He made me wait a few minutes as he hugged and talked with his faculty that were all so sad to see him go. I mean none of them had anything bad to say about him. Even some parents dropped by to let everyone know that they were going to miss him, but that they were happy that he would be waiting for their children once they got to high school. It was impressive the amount of love and respect that he received. When he finally turned to me he said in this booming voice that kind of surprised me that it came out of this short dude "John Gordon. Good to see you. What kind of team are we going to have next year?"

Mr. Hopkins was one of the best principals that I ever had. He had a way of talking to you that made you want to trust him. He did a good job of fitting into the different clicks, and he also was good at promotion and letting everyone know that things would be different at Armstrong. At the opening convocation of the division, he had us all wear orange and blue ribbons, signifying that we were the Armstrong High School faculty. I am sure that the other schools thought that he was just "showing off" instead of seeing that he was making us feel proud about the school the game and coaching the game are the same." It was like I was talking to the educational Yoda. But it made so much sense. Over the weekend I developed a practice plan that I could use like lesson plans in the classroom. He made me see the amount of time and development that I put into teaching, I had to put into coaching as well. Remember, we won six games that year, but we had a big upset win in the district tournament as the number six seed, that gave us a regional birth, and probably saved my coaching career.

Mr. Hopkins was a change agent, and I can honestly say that he improved Armstrong High School. With all the violence that was happening in the neighborhoods, enrollment was down. The same thing was occurring at John F. Kennedy High School, which didn't have as much neighborhood drama but had a lot of relatives that lived in our community, so they were getting involved too. Because of low enrollments and the systemic budget challenges that the city was facing, both schools were rumored to be combined the following year. Mr. Hopkins wanted Armstrong High School to focus on the success that was built the last couple of years, with an improving football team, and a basketball team that was currently in first place in the district. He began to look at me for additional leadership responsibilities that included acting as interim athletic director while we were attempting to fill the position. Instructionally, Mr. Hopkins invited the Virginia Department of Education to come in and review our instructional practices and provide us with tips to help our students pass the SOL's. The reviewer was to interview several teachers, those who were showing larger gains, and those who chronically were in the last quartile. During my interview, the Virginia Department of Education reviewer shared with Mr. Hopkins that he had an administrator on his teaching staff. He told Mr. Hopkins that I should be given more responsibility and that the history department should follow my instructional strategies. I couldn't believe it. Now, when the administration was out of the building, I was tapped as an administrative assistant. Bob Carter, Kassaundra Blount and I roamed the halls like we thought we were in charge. Deep down we were just happy to be out of the classroom for a day. This experience made me realize that watching everyone in an entire school was hard work. Especially when the hired staff that was supposed to do this every day laughed at us and said we were working too hard.

Eventually Mr. Hopkins became Dr. Hopkins. It impressed me that he had enough time, desire, and organizational skills to finish his doctorate while leading one of the most challenging schools in the state. Getting his doctorate done made me respect him even more. Dr. Hopkins did not back down from anyone. As the rumored merger between John F. Kennedy High School and Armstrong High School became a reality, the neighborhood tension increased dramatically. The "new" Armstrong High School would be in the John F. Kennedy building because it was newer but would keep the Armstrong name because of the history and tradition of the school. I understand why the city made the move because Armstrong only had 535 students in the 2000-2001 school year, while Kennedy had 660. If you put both schools together, you would save money and resources and be able to have athletic programs that can compete with the sure numbers that were present in all the other schools in the Central Region. The problem however, is that we now had six housing projects in the same school.

but the cafeteria. Dr. Hopkins was right in there with us. Two upperclassmen were fighting. He grabbed one, and I grabbed the other. As we were taking them up the hall to the office, the guy who Dr. Hopkins was holding tried to get at another guy who was being escorted a few steps in front of us. He lunged at the guy, and all I saw was Dr. Hopkins and him both lose their balance. I feared that Dr. Hopkins was seriously hurt due to the force with which they both hit the ground. What was even more amazing was noticing that Dr. Hopkins was uninjured, and that he never let go of the student he was escorting. He even got up first and jerked the kid off the ground and moved him even quicker to his office. I knew he was a former athlete, but you never believe it until you see it yourself. He is still a role model and friend to this day. But at the same time, that fight let me know that I couldn't stay at Armstrong any longer.

I thought that life at Meadowbrook High School would be a lot like my years as a student at Hermitage High School. As I mentioned earlier, Meadowbrook had been recently renovated and everything was new. Going to Meadowbrook High School was one of the best decisions that I ever made. When Mr. Oley introduced me to the faculty at Meadowbrook, everybody there knew I was the new basketball coach. Mr. Oley kind of threw me for a curveball when he mentioned that I had a 100 percent pass rate in history at Armstrong. A slight exaggeration, and even though I knew he said that to ease the anxiety of the department head, who was fearful that "another" coach in her department would mean someone who was more focused on winning games then passing SOL scores. Mr. Oley's boast kind of put a target on my back. I think it made some of the members of my department question exactly who I was. There were two other African-American people in the department, but they were both female. Sadly, in southern Chesterfield County, some were still threatened by an educated Black man. What I did not know is that some of these same people had filed complaints about Mr. Oley's leadership to school board members and central office directors. When I entered Meadowbrook, or MBK, as it is fondly known, I had no idea I was walking into a modern-day coup d'état. Mr. Oley had a group of faculty members that were petitioning to get him removed as principal. It was like educational politics at the highest level. Of course, I couldn't understand why because he was so supportive of me.

Mr. Oley was a pretty big guy. You can tell that he used to play football and was either a linebacker or played on the line. Some of the teachers used to say that you could tell when he was nervous or uncomfortable because he would begin to sweat. I think that he was sweating because he was just hot. Mr. Oley was like 6'3" and 275 pounds. Some teachers thought that he paid too much attention to athletics and not to improving the school. Some teachers loved him because they could tell that he was really about the kids and tried his best to keep everyone happy. That probably was the problem. There is no way to keep everyone happy, so when Mr. Oley tried, he ended up making more people unhappy. I really couldn't understand everything that he was going through until some of these same folks showed me their true colors. As I previously mentioned in this awesome book that you are reading, when I was at Armstrong High School the state Department of Education came in and provided us with several testing strategies that could potentially help the students pass their SOL tests. I always thought that one of the easier practices to implement would be conducting a review session with the students before the tests were administered. In all the proctoring protocol and testing procedures, it was made very clear that the teachers could discuss material, review, and answer student questions, if test materials had not been distributed. All teachers had an unlimited amount of time to give the test, even though we really tried to keep it to around two hours or so, so having a review was encouraged at Armstrong High School. But some of the teachers in my department never heard of this, so they accused me of cheating.

One of my colleagues in my department proctored one of my test administrations. As I began the review period before the testing window started, he sat in the back of the room with a puzzled look on his face. As students began testing, fifteen minutes or so later, he feverishly flipped through the pages of the test. When the testing was over, he didn't say anything to me, but left the room almost immediately. A few hours later, I was summoned to Mr. Oley's office. I didn't know what was going on. As I entered, Mr. Oley was in the office with the social studies department head and one of the assistant principals. Mr. Oley seemed very uncomfortable with the situation. He informed me that I had been accused of giving the students answers to the History SOL and that a full investigation would ensue. He asked me to write a statement and then return to his office. When I looked at the department head, she was literally scowling at me with anger and disgust. When I looked at the assistant principal, he could not meet my gaze. After I completed the statement, I told Mr. Oley that I wanted to go home, as tears were coming to my eyes. I couldn't believe that I was about to cry, and better yet, I couldn't believe that this was happening. It was one of those situations that I was so angry that it caused me to have tears. Mr. Oley smiled at me. He told me it was going to be okay and that he had to do his job. He also gave me advice on the perception of the situation. He said that if I went home, although it would have been my choice, the perception would have been that I was sent home because I was guilty. He was right. I had to suck it up and go teach my last class of the day like nothing ever happened. He motivated me by saying that he knows I am the type of person who wants the ball at the end of the game, and that I do not run from anything. He was Coach Oley with the way he motivated me. Pushed my buttons and said all the right things. I got through that day, taught class, and of course had to answer some questions about what the rumor mill had started. What was even more interesting was how all the black faculty members came to check on me and came to my defense. They told me the other teachers were threatened by me. They were jealous. And unfortunately, the main reason they were like that is that they were racist. A hard pill to swallow in 2002.

Meadowbrook High School used to be a predominantly white school. It was close to the country club, so that should tell you enough. But things began to change in the 1990s as more and more minorities moved in, and unfortunately a lot of the white families moved out. The faculty, however, stayed primarily white, and some of them really struggled with relating to these kids who had moved out of the city of Richmond and wanted to make a better life for themselves. Because of the change in demographics of the school, Meadowbrook became known as "Ghettobrook," and teachers complained of a lack of discipline and structure in the school. This is one of the complaints that some of those faculty members had against Mr. Oley. Realistically, Mr. Oley got along with the students well, it was the teachers who did not have the patience or were a lot quicker to write a referral for the black kids than other kids in the class. The teacher's lounge would always be a "bitchfest" for how bad this kid was in class, or how the administration was not supportive. On the day that Mr. Oley informed me that the investigation was over and that I was found to be well within the rights of a teacher on testing days, he made the mistake of laughing with me about something related to basketball in the cafeteria. By the end of the day, the rumor mill had him fixing the investigation to get me off because I was the basketball coach, and then us laughing about it in front of everyone.

I asked for a meeting with the social studies department to clear the air. I wanted the administration to be present for everything that was said so that the rumors could end. As Mr. Oley explained to the department that the review strategy that I used is perfectly legal and that it was encouraged, it was interesting to see their reactions. These teachers could not admit that they made a mistake. One teacher, who happened to serve as my mentor teacher that year, made the comment that now the paper (the *Richmond Times-Dispatch*) would show that her SOL scores would look terrible compared to mine. Another teacher came up to me and shook my hand. I was thinking that he was going to apologize, but instead he gave me some old military slogan about how I had sinned. I had *sinned?* Talk about a backhanded compliment. But the one that stood out the most was the reaction of the department head. She had the nerve to shake her head in agreement as Mr. Oley was admonishing the group for jumping to conclusions and thinking that I was guilty. I couldn't believe her. It made me so mad to watch her act like she was on my side the entire time. I finally was given the floor, and all I could really say was that I couldn't believe how many of them thought I was guilty. It wasn't everyone one of them, but the majority were white. Two of the white male teachers, who I now call friends, apologized to me on behalf of the entire group. One of them argued that they all should be following what I did if it helped increase scores. Those two shook my hand and gave me hugs. One of the black female teachers was boiling. She yelled out that this only happened because I was black. She called them racists. No one denied anything she said. I was amazed, in shock, but quickly reminded myself that although I went to white schools my entire life, I was still a black guy who some thought was nothing more than (insert any negative phrase you would like).

I think that entire episode was the final straw for Mr. Oley. Shortly afterwards, our superintendent came to one of our faculty meetings, and informed us that Mr. Oley would be moving to central office. He was going to oversee facilities and new construction since he had experience from Meadowbrook's recent renovation. During his going away speech, Mr. Oley made the following comment "Those of you who were out to get me, I forgive you. I am still going to love you, but I will never forget you." Powerful words from the man who these people thought avoided conflict like the plague. After he said that, there was a hushed silence over the room. Mr. Oley called me to his office a few days later and apologized, again, for everything that had happened to me during my first year. Even though I had a good basketball season, won 15 games and made it to the Central Region tournament, he apologized for the behavior of his staff. He told me that all the notes from the SOL investigation were coming with him and would be shredded once he got home. He wanted me to forget about it and to go on and do great things at MBK. He still calls me from time to time to check on me. He moved around some before he retired as he got tired of "central office life" and returned to be a building administrator in the private sector. He followed my basketball career and mentioned to me that he could see me doing great things. I thanked him for all his support and told him that I hope and prayed that our next principal would be as supportive as him.

Dr. Cannady, Chesterfield County's Superintendent of Schools at the time, came to one of our faculty meetings again within the next couple of weeks. We heard rumors of who our next principal was going to be, but nothing would be made concrete until he/she walked through those doors. Dr. Cannady introduced us to Mr. Jeff Ellick, who was the current principal at Manchester Middle School. I had a little bit of deja-vu as I was having another high school principal of mine being replaced by a middle school principal that I heard good things about, but did not have high school experience. Mr. Ellick was also an African-American man, and in looking at the history of Meadowbrook's principals, I believe he was the first African-American principal in school history. I fondly remember him giving his speech to the student body a few short days later, and he explained to them that he wanted to have order and structure, but he also wanted the students to have fun during their stay at MBK. His speech to the students was much better than his speech to the faculty, in which he rambled a little bit while trying to contain his excitement about this new position. The faculty was relieved that Mr. Oley was no longer going to be there, but they were a little uneasy about having someone in charge that did not have any high school experience. Once again, they were wrong. If they had done just a little bit of research, they would have known that Mr. Ellick was an assistant principal at Manchester High School for years before he became a middle school principal. That is one thing about the rumor mill in education. If one of the more respected members of the faculty repeats any type of rumor, then it is considered gospel by everyone else.

Mr. Ellick was well respected by the people in central office. He did a very good job of building relationships with staff and promoting leadership within the building. One of the first things that he noticed, and mentioned to some of us, is that he was amazed at how the make-up of the faculty was not representative of the make-up of the student body. He also mentioned how he would have to be careful in addressing this issue. Mr. Ellick had a plan. He was going to spend his first year doing a lot of observation, seeing who the major players were, and making subtle changes to make the school better. He decided that he would create deans of students in the building to help the administration with discipline. The theory was based on the Deans handling most if not all of the discipline, which would then free up the assistant principals to focus more on the instructional side of their jobs. To become a dean of students, you had to be enrolled in an administration and supervision program, or in the process of being enrolled. He picked two of our younger teachers to serve in this role. This irritated some of the faculty members because they did not believe that these two teachers had been in the classroom long enough and may not have the respect of the "veteran" teachers. Mr. Ellick saw leadership in these two and had a conversation with me about becoming a dean as well. I was more interested in coaching basketball, but did have some interest in being the assistant athletic director because that position was more than likely going to be open because our current athletic director was retiring. Our assistant AD was the leading candidate to replace him. When I told him I was interested in being the assistant AD, he was kind of surprised because he thought I was coming to talk to him about being the athletic director. He already had his well-rehearsed response of "She will be a candidate" locked and loaded, and then he paused when I told him my intentions, smiled at me, and said, "John Gordon, I think we can make that happen."

Mr. Ellick got initiated by fire during his brief tenure as the principal at Meadowbrook High School. Unfortunately, he experienced one of the greatest fears of being an administrator, by having one of your students die while attending school. This tragedy happened after school, as one of our students was crossing the street on his way home and was struck by a car. Mr. Ellick handled it with great calm and demeanor. He led efforts to have the street named after the student and of course put additional safety measures in place to hopefully prevent something like that from happening again. Mr. Ellick also made additional changes in our leadership structure as he brought in new assistant principals, promoted one of the deans to an assistant principal, and began to change the culture of the school.

One of the main things I learned from Mr. Ellick is the importance of order. From his perspective, having a student altercation, where large crowds of students would go out of their way to get a better view created chaos. Any time we had an altercation, Mr. Ellick would come over the PA system and re-explain the rule about fighting at Meadowbrook High School. The part that rang true more than any is when he reminded the students that if you fight at Meadowbrook, you would no longer attend Meadowbrook. I don't know how he did it, but he kept his word. Students who were involved in altercations were removed and placed in alternative school. Mr. Ellick sent the strong message that he was strong on discipline, consistent in his message, and that he wanted students to be able to come to school and not worry about stuff like that. The student body didn't like it at first but came to respect the message and abided by the rules. The faculty also felt they were being supported. Mr. Ellick did a great job of having both the faculty and the students on his side. Things were going great at school and we were ending the stereotypical name of "Ghettobrook."

But as the old cliché says, "All good things must come to an end." Mr. Ellick called an emergency faculty meeting mid-year. Dr. Cannady was there again, and we had no idea what to expect. Mr. Ellick announced that he had gotten the call. We all were like, call from whom, as we had no idea what he was talking about. He clarified his words, by saying Uncle Sam had called and that he had to go. None of us knew that he was in the US Army Reserves. He had been called to active duty in Afghanistan and would be taking a leave of absence. He informed us that he had no idea how long he would be gone, but that he would be thinking about us every day. The faculty was in shock. A few shed some tears, which was even more shocking. Dr. Cannady then closed out the meeting and introduced us to Mr. Neal Fletcher, assistant principal at Matoaca High School, who would serve as interim principal in Mr. Ellick's absence.

I met Mr. Fletcher while he was an assistant principal at Matoaca High School when he visited Meadowbrook during an administrative training. He came up to me to let me know that he really liked how my staff and my players carried themselves at basketball games. He said that besides the fact that we were winning games, we presented ourselves in a very professional manner, the players wore shirt and ties to games, and all the coaches looked like GQ models on the sidelines. I thought it was nice for him to say that, especially after we had just beaten Matoaca handily the night before. Mr. Fletcher was a people's person. He got along with everyone and had a great sense of humor. He had been an assistant principal in several different school divisions for over a decade, after a stint in the military. Like Jeff Ellick, he was a fraternity brother of mine, and when he was named principal, we hit it off instantly.

I understand that Dr. Cannady chose Mr. Fletcher to serve as interim principal partly because he was another African-American man, but also because he wanted to give him an opportunity to expand his leadership skills and prove that he could run his own building. From what we were originally told, Mr. Fletcher would serve in this capacity until Mr. Ellick returned, which was supposed to have been by the end of the year. As many of the staff members were continuing to send Mr. Ellick care packages, and videos of events at school, the question always came back to "When is Mr. Ellick coming back?" When I asked Neal the same question, he looked at me in a puzzled way and said, "I don't know when he is coming back, or what he is coming back to." I then realized that Mr. Fletcher had done a solid enough of a job that Dr. Cannady had decided to keep him in the position permanently. When this news got out, it kind of gave some of our faculty members an uneasy feeling, but they still had not made their minds up about Mr. Fletcher.

The students loved Mr. Fletcher. I learned from him the importance of "MBWA" or managing by wandering around. He was always very visible in the halls, did a great job of carrying on conversations and building relationships with students, and showing the students respect. That was the hard part for some of the staff members to deal with. Some of the same teachers who felt they ran Mr. Oley out of the building and were nervous about Mr. Ellick because they thought he did not have enough high school experience felt that Mr. Fletcher sided with the students too much. Of course, my first inclination was to believe that they were just being this way because of their semi-racist overtures, but then I realized that some of these teachers just did not like being told what to do if they did not agree with it.

Mr. Fletcher realized that a lot of the issues that occurred at MBK were due to the faculty's inability to relate to and build relationships with the students. At faculty meetings, he would continue to preach about the importance of getting to know your students, and to attend their concerts

and contests to help alleviate some of the discipline problems that could occur in their classes. It was no secret that
a lot of the faculty had less patience with the black students
than they had with their white counterparts. There was
also a divide with the faculty and staff that taught solely in
the International Baccalaureate Programme because they
thought they should have a different set of rules and expectations than the rest of the school. Mr. Fletcher believed
that even though we had this great instructional program
for all students in our building, we needed to have the same
philosophy, policies, and attitudes for everyone. A noble
cause at best.

Many of the IB teachers thought they were smarter than
Mr. Fletcher. They would try to maneuver around him to
get things done that would only benefit the IB students.
Some of the cutthroat tactics included having some of
our more predominant families question him on things
to school board members and to central office personnel.
Mr. Fletcher explained that he wanted what was best for all
students and not just the 150 students who were in the IB
program. For a while, things became pretty cutthroat on a
day-to-day basis, and Neal Fletcher was always looking for
someone who he could trust. When Mr. Ellick returned
from his tour of duty and was placed at a middle school,
some vacancies began to pop up as some of our administrators and teachers requested transfers to his school. It was
interesting that some of the same teachers who questioned
Mr. Ellick when he was our principal now suddenly wanted to go work with him. That was fine with Mr. Fletcher
because he knew those that left did not support him anyway. I can remember when one of the Dean of Students

positions came open, he called me over the summer and asked me to come in and interview for it. I had no interest. I was having a successful stint as basketball coach and my players I was grooming for three years were now rising seniors. He told me over the phone that I would still be able to coach basketball and be a Dean. I wouldn't have to teach classes and I would no longer have to answer to the history department head. I talked to my wife about it and decided to take the plunge. It ended up being a great decision.

What I did not expect was how some of the teachers treated me since I was now an administrator. I oversaw science, world languages, custodians, security, and the maintenance of the building. One of the first conflicts that I had to deal with was a world language teacher who decided to reduce her hours and become part-time. Due to her being a part-time teacher, she no longer would have access to the laptop that we gave her during her full-time role. This was county policy. Regardless of how many times I asked her to turn her laptop into the library so that we could redistribute it to another staff member, she would create excuses, lie, or just balk at my authority. Finally, when I threatened to have her written up, she stormed into Mr. Fletcher's office and said that I would get her laptop "over her dead body" and that someone needed to "bring me down a notch" because she didn't know "who I think I am." Damn. I was just doing my job. She ended up resigning shortly after that to go back to be a stay-at-home mom.

Because I was now an administrator, some people viewed me as a threat. The current athletic director could not believe that I was now an administrator. When I served as her assistant, she made sure she gave me the most disrespectful jobs she could find. She asked me to work in the concession stand during JV football games. I did not have a big problem with this request, except for the fact that it was August, and the concession stand doors had been closed all day. The inside temperature was easily 120 degrees. When we explained to her how hot it was in there, and if we could open the doors for an hour or so before we started so it could cool down, she would always deny our request and make comments like, "If you don't like the jobs I give you, you can always let Mr. Fletcher know that you are resigning from your position." That was her goal: to get me to quit. The funny part was that the other assistant AD, an older white guy who was nice, was always placed at the front gate greeting people for games and helping manage the ticket-takers. She never switched our positions. I knew what she was trying to do, and I was not going to let her force me to quit. But what she did not know is that I kept a written record of everything she did that I thought was deliberately done to hurt my basketball program or me personally.

When I was named dean of students, this AD went to Mr. Fletcher and told him that she thought it was a mistake. She explained that my basketball players would get special treatment and people would not take me seriously because I was the basketball coach. Mr. Fletcher expected this from her. He had already gotten on her because she refused to purchase uniforms and resources for the soccer team. I think she made this decision because the soccer team was primarily composed of Hispanic players. She would do any and everything for the football and baseball teams, but sports like basketball and soccer were left to fend for themselves. The basketball program was self-sufficient, as I had

school of over 1700 students is the most difficult task for an administrator. Luckily, I had great training from the "Master Schedule Guru" Mrs. Kay Lawson, who was so knowledgeable and very nice. She showed me how to manipulate sections and seat counts using our student management system Starbase, and how to project growth in certain subjects and grade levels. I could not have done this without her. When the central office subject specialists, directors, and others came to Mr. Fletcher asking questions on why the courses were created this way, I was ready and organized. After a few meetings on the creation of some changes that we had to implement due to increasing the seat time in our school day, creating a study period at the end of one of our blocks, and the creation of new classes, they left us alone, satisfied that we knew what we were doing. Mr. Fletcher was very appreciative of the work I did and promoted me to an assistant principal the following year.

I thought things were different when I became a dean, they were even more intense as an assistant principal. In my new role, even though I had less experience, I was the assistant principal that ran the building in Mr. Fletcher's absence. Part of this decision was because our other two assistant principals were new to the building and were learning the MBK culture and politics that come along with being in a leadership position. Mr. Fletcher gave me full reign to do whatever I thought was necessary to make the building successful. He allowed me to purchase new décor for the building including welcome mats, signs, school spirit paintings, etc. The school looked marvelous! (In my Billy Crystal voice from the Saturday night live skits!) The teachers and school community really appreciated the work being done, and we had a great administrative team that worked so well together. But for some, this was an issue. As we know humans are creatures of habit, and because our faculty was used to dysfunction, I am not sure if they liked the fact that we were getting along so well. As I mentioned earlier, the faculty at Meadowbrook was used to being able to manipulate administrators and other school personnel to create infighting and bickering. Mr. Fletcher believed that some of the teachers unfortunately had issues taking directives from people of color. Five out of our seven administrators were African-American. This had never happened at Meadowbrook before. Ideally, in the field of education, the faculty and staff should be a direct representation of the student body that it serves. Mr. Fletcher was big on this, and he did a tremendous job of providing more of our minority students with teachers who may have a better chance of being role models because they looked like the students. Some of the faculty were threatened by this concept as well. In the end, some of the pushback or potential backstabbing that was going on could have been due to race. This was extremely sad, since the faculty and staff was serving a population that was approximately 75% minority.

Three years as a teacher, two years as a dean, and one year as an assistant principal. That was a pretty quick ascension in one building, and some may have thought I had moved too fast or only got promoted because I was the "principal's boy." What many of them did not know is that I almost turned down my role as an assistant principal because of the compensation policy of Chesterfield County Public Schools stated that an assistant principal could not receive an athletic stipend due to their paid role for the supervision of athletic events. This meant that I could make the choice to continue coaching basketball, but that I would have to do it for free. This information was given to me in August. Now, as a basketball coach, I worked year-round on perfecting my craft and developing my players. By August, we only had three months before the season started, and I could not see myself walking away at that time and basically turning my back on my players. That and the fact that we had suffered through my only losing season the previous year. Being the head coach and an administrator was nothing new in Chesterfield as Mr. Fletcher checked with the principal at Thomas Dale High School to see how he worked everything out with his soccer coach, who also served as an assistant principal. The county would allow me to coach, but now I had to explain to my family that all the hours that I put in to building a successful program would continue, but there would not be any financial compensation for my work. It was a tough conversation, but Shavonne knew that I loved the game of basketball so much, I would have done it for free anyway.

My last year of coaching kind of became a retirement tour, winning seventeen games, but not advancing like we would like. I cried when my season ended in the district tournament with a one-point loss to Thomas Dale. My best player dribbled the ball off his foot when going in for a contested layup with two seconds remaining on the clock. That loss still hurts to this day. At the end of the school year, I decided that it was going to be too difficult to remain at Meadowbrook and not be the basketball coach. Even though being an assistant principal was my chief role and responsibility, Coach Gordon was a huge part of my identity. I spoke with Dr. Lyle Evans, Asst. Superintendent for Chesterfield County Public Schools, and requested a transfer to Monacan High School.

The principal of Monacan High School was David Sovine. Dave was very well respected throughout the county as he had done tremendous jobs in his two middle school stints as principal. Dr. Cannady came to Dave one day and asked him to take on Monacan as a school that had so much potential but needed to improve their overall structure. Dave, who wanted to be a superintendent in his own right, loved the challenge. Monacan High School is tucked away in the back of the Smoketree neighborhood and was one of Chesterfield County's first planned communities. The school lot is adjacent to one of the elementary schools and had a school design that was very prevalent throughout the Central Region of Virginia. Under Mr. Sovine, Monacan began to be recognized as one of the top high schools in the state due to strong instructional programs and the growth of the Humanities program as the school's specialty center. The athletic programs at Monacan were generally competitive and the school was recently coming off a state championship in baseball. Mr. Sovine's reputation as a strong instructional leader was well known throughout the county, and he was part of the "triumvirate" of high school principals along with Pete Koste from Manchester High School and John Titus from James River High School. The triumvirate was looked upon as being very wise and in many ways helping to set school policy for the rest of the county.

When Dr. Evans spoke to me about the possibility of going to Monacan High School, I was excited to learn some new things and to see if Monacan was that different from Meadowbrook High School. This was also going to be my first time being in a high school setting and not being the basketball coach. Monacan was totally different than both Meadowbrook and Armstrong High Schools. The students generally did everything that was asked of them and the faculty respected the principal. The main difference was the demographic breakdown of the faculty itself. I quickly noticed that I was the only African-American male in the entire building. Well, besides the one custodian, Norman. I could not believe that a school that was approximately 35 percent African-American did not have any African-American male role models for the students. There were approximately eight African-American staff members who made sure that they reminded me of the importance of my presence there. When I spoke to Dr. Evans about this issue, he said it was being addressed and that I was the first piece of the puzzle. I must admit that when it feels like you have the weight of an entire race on your shoulders, it can be a little overwhelming.

Walking the halls at Monacan let me know that the African-American men were craving my attention or other role models. There were numerous incidents daily when the ninth-grade students who I worked with received discipline referrals in and they would claim the teacher was picking on them or did not understand them. How could I argue when I looked at the referral and the student was sent out for talking but may or may not have been given a warning. Did some of the same issues that the teachers at Meadowbrook had with not having patience for students of color also apply at Monacan? When I brought these same concerns to Mr. Sovine, he truly understood this was something that needed to be addressed and he allowed me to lead some professional development on this topic. I think to this day it was well received, but we knew it would be very difficult to change that culture in a short period of time.

I also suggested that we needed to get some African-American male teachers on the faculty at Monacan. Dave explained to me they had very few candidates over the years, and he had not interviewed one in a while. I can remember him speaking with the Human Resources department anytime we had a vacancy and making it very clear he wanted the "best of the best" when it came to candidates. (There's that '80s movie reference again.) I know being the best did not mean you had to be white, but it meant that you had to know your craft and be a good fit for the school. These candidates had to be out there, right? I found it very hard to swallow because due to the previous three years in which I served on the administrative team at Meadowbrook, over half of the candidates were black. I began to think that the cultural divide that occurred between the eastern and western parts of the county also helped to dictate what type of candidates applied or were sent for certain jobs. You see, Meadowbrook was on the eastern side of the county, closer to the City of Richmond, and as a result had larger minority populations. Monacan was more on the western side of the county, and in many areas was considered "old Chesterfield" or the traditional part of the county. With a school where diversity was becoming more prevalent within the population, the need for more minority faculty was becoming more and more necessary. That was really the only regret I had during my one year at

Monacan High School. I wish I could have made a greater difference in bringing more minority professional staff to the building.

Dave Sovine was very strong on instruction. In many ways, a lot of the instructional strategies I used during my tenure as principal were borrowed and tweaked from my time with him. He did a tremendous job of using data to drive instruction and developed enrichment programs to help our achievement gap with our different subgroups. The year I arrived at Monacan was also the year that we started "Monacan Morning," which was a thirty-minute enrichment period at the beginning of the school day. "Monacan Morning" allowed the students to get extra help, make up work, and complete assessments without taking away from their daily instructional time. Genius! It took a little time to get the kids to understand the importance of attending the program, but they soon found out it would be a greater help in the long run.

For the teachers, it was a little bit of a different story. Some of them believed that adding this enrichment period put more work on their plate. They were not like the Meadowbrook staff, who took their concerns out of the building. Instead they would set up meetings with the administration to voice their concerns. In the end, their professionalism came through, and I can honestly say that they implemented the program with fidelity. Dave was very appreciative of the faculty and would find small ways to show it like providing additional meals for the staff throughout the school year. He always explained to me that he believed in getting to know people and treating them with respect. One of the first conversations he had with me was Monacan's version of radio protocol. We weren't going to use numbers or codes when addressing someone; we would call them by their name, because they were people. I can still hear him saying it now: People. That is the only way to grow your building and your culture: by dealing with people in a professional and respectable manner.

I didn't know that some of the staff feared Dave. For about two weeks, we had a small problem with some of the staff members being late to work for their first period class. They weren't real late, but it seemed they would be rushing in as the kids were coming in and were unpacking as the kids were writing down the daily bell ringer that was jotted down on the board. When Dave noticed this happening a little too much to his liking, he decided he was going to stand in the parking lot the next day with a clipboard and note when each staff member arrived. He still greeted people in his normal pleasant manner but wrote down their time. He never had to follow up with anyone for being late again, as the message was received loud and clear. The discussions of the teachers noticing that he was in the parking lot was priceless, and their fear of having a letter placed in their files was even greater. He didn't have to say a word for his point to get across. That is respect, or power, or even fear. To me it just showed another way to accomplish a goal without making unnecessary noise about it.

Dave had his own career goals and privately began to look for other leadership opportunities. He had just received his doctorate degree from the University of Virginia, and now had goals of becoming a superintendent. His prior relationships he had with other educational leaders across the state were second to none. We found out on graduation day he was not going to be returning to Monacan High School. I overheard the conversation as one of the Asst. Superintendents was having a conversation with Dave and a few others, and she made the comment that he was going to be a principal for at least "one more day!" I could tell he was uncomfortable that the news had gotten out, as I am sure he wanted to tell us in his own way and at the right time. He leaned in and clarified to the other high-ranking school official that he'd just accepted a job as the executive director of secondary education for Spotsylvania County Schools. After graduation, Dave took the entire administrative team out for dinner to celebrate having a great year. He and I never mentioned what I overheard, but he did address the team on his intentions the next day. Dave was very professional in relaying the information to us, and I could tell that at least one of the other administrators knew it was coming. What we did not expect was the lobbying that would begin the very next day as the faculty received the news that afternoon.

Monacan had three very capable assistant principals, including myself, who were interested in becoming the principal. Two of us had only been there for one year, while the third had been there since Dave arrived. Even though she was the "senior" administrator by both age and experience, she was not well liked or respected by the faculty. This caused the faculty to begin to feel the need to approach me and gauge my interest. They offered to write letters to the superintendent on my behalf. They asked to be a part of the interview panel. Parents began to inquire as to which one of us would take over. At our annual golf tournament, which raised tens of thousands of dollars in scholarship money and other resources for the school, the foursome I was playing with kept reinforcing that I should be the next principal. They complimented me on how I made such a huge difference in one year, and that they knew the community would get behind me. I made the mistake of feeding into some of this support, and I began to encourage faculty members to write letters on my behalf to the superintendent if they thought it would help. Of course, within a school, the rumor mill turned that into me "asking" people to write letters. This made the supporters of our veteran assistant principal feel outraged and slighted. The next thing you know, a petition was circulating around the building in support of her "candidacy for principal." I had no idea this would become an election.

I am sure that with the academic reputation of Monacan High School being what it was, there were several candidates who applied for the position. My interview went well, and I was chosen as a finalist, and was asked to have my final interview with the superintendent, Dr. Newsome. I later discovered that the two other assistant principals were asked to meet with Dr. Newsome as well. Now wait a minute! Could it be possible that all three of us were finalists for the same position? As my sources began to dig even more, (I told you this became an election and then a covert operation), word spread that there was also a mysterious fourth candidate. Who was this person? And how dare they invade on this educational soap opera that we had going on in relation to the Monacan principal position?

During my meeting with Dr. Newsome, and later in my discussion with Dr. Evans, I was informed that there were only two finalists: me and the mysterious fourth candidate. Dr. Newsome wanted to meet with the other assistant principals/candidates to gauge if they would be able to follow someone else within the building if they were not the successful candidate. Talk about a tough conversation. Dr. Newsome also informed me that the school board member for Monacan's zone had some reservations about me becoming the principal. It was not based on anything regarding my ability, but it was completely based on the color of my skin. This school board member told Dr. Newsome that she wanted to preserve the history and tradition of Monacan High School when it came to that position. Now, we all know that was code for "We do not want this African-American individual to run our school." I did not know at the time that I would have become the first African-American principal in Monacan High School History. I know this must have weighed heavily on Dr. Newsome's mind, and I also feel thankful that he felt comfortable enough to share that with me. However, I also had a plan B in case things did not work out. Secretly, I was also a finalist for the principal position at James Monroe High School in Fredericksburg, Virginia. The irony of it all was that Dr. Evans was the person who brought the James Monroe vacancy to my attention. I interviewed for James Monroe two weeks after I interviewed for Monacan, and Fredericksburg moved pretty quickly in the process. When I called Dr. Evans to discuss the fact that James Monroe had just offered me the position, Dr. Evans told me that the superintendent was still splitting hairs over this decision. I then asked Dr. Evans about the potential salary for

Chapter 6

Principal Qualities and Characteristics

Listed below are nine characteristics that are positive qualities of good principals. Please rank these qualities from one to ten, with one being the most important, and ten being the least important. Please discuss your top and bottom three qualities with members of your book group or your colleagues.

_____ Ability to Build Relationships

_____ Being Approachable

_____ Communication Skills

_____ Consistency

_____ Knowledge of the School Community

_____ Organizational Skills

_____ School Improvement

_____ Transparency

_____ Visibility

_____ Years of Experience

JM welcomes first black principal

BY HUGH MUIR
THE FREE LANCE-STAR

John B. Gordon III is the new principal at James Monroe High School, and the city school's first African–American leader.

A basketball shooting guard who set a game record for 3-pointers (six) as a senior at Richmond's Hermitage High, Gordon coached high school teams to numerous titles over 13 years. He taught history and social studies before "crossing the desk" in 2005 to become an administrator.

Born in Richmond, Gordon will be 36 on Aug. 23. He lives in Henrico County with his wife, Shavonne, also a Richmond native, whom he met while both were first-year students at the University of Virginia. They have three children: Marcus, who is studying forensic chemistry at Longwood University in Farmville; Kennedy ("We call

John B. Gordon III of Richmond is the new principal at James Monroe High School in Fredericksburg.

her 'Ken' "), 5; and Simone, 6 months.

"I had always wanted to coach basketball," Gordon said, "but my mother [Marian, an elementary school principal] told me early on, 'If you want to coach, you have to be a teacher.' "

His father had been the third African–American to attend U.Va., and Gordon followed him to Charlottesville. He majored in psychology and graduated in 1995.

Gordon earned a master's in education from U.Va. in 2000 and a post-master's in education administration and supervision from Virginia Commonwealth University in 2007. He is working on a doctorate in educational leadership and policy at Virginia Tech.

Shavonne graduated from U.Va. as a systems engineer and got a job in Delaware with

SEE PRINCIPAL, PAGE 3

This article in the *Free-Lance Star* was one of the best moments of my career. I had officially arrived as a principal! I wished the article would have spoken more about my vision as an instructional leader than my career as a basketball coach.

Chapter 7

My Administration

I did it. I had finally become a principal. It was my dream to run my own high school and put into place some of the good ideas that I learned along the way. In chapter 6, I detailed characteristics of the principals I worked with, hoping to cultivate all the good things that a high school needs to be successful. I had a simple plan of making sure the students respected the school and knew that I was approachable, but also took pride in everything that related to their high school experience. James Monroe High School (JMHS) in Fredericksburg, Virginia had a great reputation of being a strong academic and athletic school. When I took over in 2009, JMHS was coming off a state championship in football and had strong SOL scores in the mid and upper eighties, but needed a culture change as it related to discipline. One of the first things I did when I became principal was contact every faculty member on staff and I ask them, "If you could change one thing at JM, what would it be?" Over 60 percent of the faculty stated that tardies were an issue. I was thinking, that's it? Fixing tardies would not be a problem at all. Neal Fletcher had a similar issue at Meadowbrook High School, and he instituted clean sweeps. OMG! The Clean Sweep. To some, it was like I had brought nuclear weapons to Fredericksburg, Virginia. The Clean Sweep Policy was as follows:

Once the tardy bell rang, teachers would be instructed via the PA to close and lock their doors. Any students remaining in the halls would be brought to the commons area to receive their discipline accordingly.

What did that word accordingly mean? In my mind, it meant that the school administration, Mrs. Cavataio, Mrs. Rachal, and I could give whatever we thought to be the necessary discipline for these routine rule breakers. I got a quick lesson on policy and protocol when I did not spell out what accordingly meant. I learned that parents and the school community wanted to know exactly what would happen to their children if they were caught in the God-forbidden clean sweep. Of course, I had a large percentage of parents who thought it was too harsh, that it should go away, and that tardies were not that big of a deal. Some parents argued that we were causing their children to miss even more instructional time because we brought them to the commons for consequences. I also learned that some of these same parents had direct lines to our school board members, who in turn would relay these concerns to our superintendent, Dr. Melton. I can remember him telling me, "I am tired of hearing about clean sweeps." You see, Dr. Melton understood the necessity of having strong discipline at a high school, as he was a former high school principal himself. He just wasn't sure how our school community was going to react to a radical idea of locking kids out of class and giving them discipline as you see fit.

Dr. Melton sent my central office liaison Bob Burch to see me in September to discuss clean sweeps. Mr. Burch was a former principal of James Monroe High School and loved the school dearly. He was a big supporter of mine and always tried to protect me, but also was there to tell me when I was wrong. The faculty loved the clean sweeps—that was, until one of their own children happened to be caught in one. The plan was very simple: I would give the students a week to learn their way around the school, fall into a routine, and then remind them that tardies were unacceptable at James Monroe High School. When we did our first clean sweep, approximately forty kids were caught. What made this so controversial was that some of the more popular kids in school that were late that day: football players, cheerleaders, even some members of the National Honor Society. When my administration and I made the calls to the parents saying that some kids had in-school suspension, and some (because they were repeat offenders) had multiple days, you would have thought I'd shot the Pope.

The football coach was mad because his players might have to miss a game, and parents were mad because being caught in the clean sweep meant that it would be a discipline infraction that would be placed in their file and could prevent them from earning admission into the college of their choice. Wow. All because of a tardy? Mr. Burch informed me that I had to create a discipline matrix of what would happen if a student was caught in a clean sweep so parents would know the consequences. "Will be disciplined accordingly" had to go away because it was too broad and not specific. Even though we still ran into some issues with consequences for clean sweeps, it proved to be a step in the right direction.

You always hear the age-old saying that you don't know what it is like to be principal until you are a principal. That saying sure is true. It is a little different when you know that the buck stops here and that you are going to be the final decision maker on everything. It also means that you are going to have to deal with things that are not in any of the textbooks that you read and studied in your educational leadership classes. As I mentioned in the beginning of this chapter, James Monroe High School was coming off a state championship in football when I arrived. Expectations were high for the football program again that year due to several starters returning from the championship football team. The football coach, who also served as the athletic director, was the face of the athletic program, and he knew that he was going to be good. The team lost their first game of the year, but then rattled off like eight wins straight.

Then all hell broke loose. Word had begun to spread throughout the community that JM had an ineligible player on the team. This story originated with a disgruntled parent who was mad that their son was not getting any playing time. The parent did not like the football coach and decided the best way to get back at him was to put this information out into the school community. After the football coach/athletic director got wind of this information, he and I sat down to determine if these allegations were indeed true. I asked him how he validated if students were eligible for each season. He explained to me that he checked the report cards at the end of each school year and then cross-referenced their grades with the standards that were set by the Virginia High School League. I then asked how he confirmed years of eligibility, since a potential student athlete could only compete for four years, or eight semesters maximum. This was where the mistake was made. The football coach explained that he asked all students when they started school, and based on their response, he took their word for it. The student in question was in his fifth year of high school eligibility. The football coach/athletic director did not review the student's start date before the season started. Now, this student athlete was not an impact player and rarely even participated in any of the games. We would call him a benchwarmer. But the problem was, this benchwarmer was on the master eligibility list and participated in four or five games because they were blowouts. This was a scandal, and a public relations nightmare that no first-year principal should have to deal with.

When I had to report this information to the Virginia High School League (VHSL), it was one of the most difficult things I had to do. I explained this error was due to a record-keeping mistake from our athletic department and that we asked for leniency in judgement since we were 8-1 with one game remaining on the schedule. At the time, we were also number two in our region as we prepared for the post-season. At the high school level, the start of the school year strongly depends on the excellence of your football program. Going from 8-1 to 0-9 would be a catastrophic event that would be like all the Jedi being executed by the Emperor in the Star Wars movies. When our football coach held the meeting with his players to break the bad news that we had to forfeit all our games, it was like a funeral. Several football players just left the building. We tried to talk to them and remind them that school is more important than just playing football, but it fell on deaf ears. Most of them eventually calmed down, but their parents wanted to do everything under the sun to try and see if the VHSL would change their decision. I received dozens of phone calls and e-mails encouraging me to appeal the decision. I explained to as many parents and supporters as I could that this mistake was James Monroe High School's mistake and ours alone, and the appeal would not be in our favor. I even caught a lot of flak because I committed to traveling to the tidewater area to support our Girls' Field Hockey Team that was competing for a State Championship instead of staying in my office and working the lines with the VHSL. What people did not know was that I was on the phone with the VHSL for the two-and-a-half-hour commute to the field hockey championships. When I returned to work the next day, I had at least ten messages and three meetings set up by parents who wanted something to be done about this. The word "death penalty" was now being thrown around, and James Monroe High School football was being compared to SMU football from the 1980s.

During this time, I was vice chairman of Region I of the VHSL and had a very good relationship with the VHSL staff. Also, due to the number of appeals that I heard and being part of the deliberation process, I knew there was no way in hell our appeal was going to be successful. However, due to our school community being adamant that we at least try, I went forward with guns blazing, including interviews, testimonials from the football coach/athletic director, and political support from very influential people in our community. The appeal committee was very understanding and very complimentary of the football coach, who many of the members knew personally. However, our appeal was unanimously denied. This created some tension between the influential members of our community and the VHSL staff. Many of our community members wanted the executive director of the VHSL fired, saying that he was being unreasonable and kids should not be punished for mistakes made by adults. Point taken. The student who lied about being a fifth-year student was forced to move away due to death threats to him and his family. Football is taken very seriously in Fredericksburg. I also thought the football coach was going to resign from his position as athletic director, but then the strangest thing occurred on senior night, which is the last home football game of the year. The same fans who were calling for the football coach to be fired and removed from being athletic director cheered his name for the last two minutes of the fourth quarter. It was like we were at a professional wrestling match for the WWE, and the fans were chanting his name like they do for the Rock. It was amazing. I also realized that the football coach probably had more political capital in this school community than me and the superintendent combined.

At the fall sports banquet and graduation speeches that year, I mentioned how the football team and community rallied together for the last game of the season. Of course, it was a victory, or I would not have mentioned it. We graduated on the same field that the football team played their last game. As I said, football is taken very seriously in Fredericksburg and I know the topic still hurts many to this day. I was so proud of how the student athletes had grown up during those tough times, and I know it made all of them better people today.

Many of the players who were juniors developed a strong bond with me because they felt I had their backs and was in the trenches with them. They quoted aspects of the speech that I gave them on the day that we delivered the bad news that they had to forfeit eight games. I also think they began to do their own research on me and detailed aspects of my basketball coaching background. They now saw me as one of them, and hopefully as a role model to what they aspired to become. It is funny how tough times really bring people together and helps to develop life-long relationships. It is still unfortunate that the players had to go through that to become closer.

We ended up going to the state championship football game a total of three times during my five-year stint as the principal at James Monroe High School but could not get over the championship hump. Overall, our athletic programs improved tremendously during my tenure. I would always say that I wanted our athletic program to be known as more than just a football school. I wanted all of our programs to be the best of the best. (There it is again!) I remembered reading articles about the University of Florida and how their athletic department wanted to be a national champion in every sport. For this to happen, there needed to be a culture of excellence in everything that they did. That article really hit home for me. I wanted James Monroe High School to be the best in everything, too. I remembered listening to Bob Burch and several other community members about how special a place James Monroe High School was, and how there is no other place like it. That is when it hit me. We weren't going to be like other high schools. We weren't even going to be like the three other James Monroe High Schools in America. We were now going to be known as *The* James Monroe High School.

explained to our students, we are a special place. You are lucky to attend our school. Make the most of it. We believe in excellence. We have school pride. We are the one high school in the United States of America that believes in being excellent in everything we do. The students bought into it.

At graduation during my second year as principal, I explained to everyone what the *The* meant. I remember giving the speech and providing credit to Mr. Bob Burch for being the one who inspired me to come up with the idea. As I stated before, no one has more pride or loves that school more than Bob Burch. Well maybe Charlie McDaniel, who could be a close second. In the speech, I let everyone know that adding the was more than a play on words, because each letter meant something. The T stood for togetherness. *The* James Monroe High School community was very diverse. Students and families that came from all walks of life. Different socioeconomic statuses, different learning styles, but everyone would come together to support our sports teams and the belief that the school was the flagship of the division. The H stood for the rich history that James Monroe High School had over the years. From both the academic and athletic accomplishments, to the generations upon generations that attended. When the old building was taken down and the current building was being built, Bob Burch told me stories of the auction that took place during the renovation. People bought the urinals from the locker rooms. Yes, you read that right: the urinals that were used for over fifty years. Purchased, carried out with pride, and placed in the back of a truck or car. My next question was, what do you do with it when you get home? Do you have it installed? Does the urinal have some special sentimental meaning to the buyers? How do you explain it to your wife or your significant other? Lastly, we all know that when you were removing it from the wall, it had not been cleaned yet. Wow.

Anyway, it really was an example of how much people loved that school, and how the history is so appreciated. The E stood for the excellence in education that was the foundation for Fredericksburg City Public Schools. *The* James Monroe High School was going to be the school that could win the state football championship, academic bowl, and obtain the blue-ribbon status in performing arts. We were going to be excellent. In everything. When I finished the speech at graduation, dozens of people came up to me afterwards explaining that they had always wondered what the the meant or that they had no idea that it was an acronym for something else. *The* James Monroe High School was more than a marketing or branding idea. It was a change in culture in wanting to be the best in everything. It raised the standard to being excellent, in challenging all students to get involved in school, and increasing the sense of school pride that would bridge generations. Mission accomplished.

It is usually said that in your second year of leadership, you begin to put your stamp on things and change the things that you did not like or did not agree with during your first year of observation. For me, it was all about changing the persona of James Monroe High School as it relates to building personality. *The* James Monroe High School would scream "school spirit" as soon as you stepped foot on campus. When I first entered "JM" I was very appreciative of its architecture, design, and spacious places for gathering.

What I did not like was the fact that it was so plain, looked like a hospital, and had no personality. Over the summer we received a life-sized copy of the school mission statement from *Lifetouch*. I decided to have this placed on the bare wall near the office so that everyone would see it as soon as you entered the building. I also decided to add the parking lot flags with a new logo that I made up one weekend when driving home. Living in Glen Allen and working in Fredericksburg had its challenges at times, but it did allow me to think, process, and brainstorm a lot of new ideas, since I had a 45-minute commute. My goal was to then create new building improvement projects that would give the students something new to look forward to every year.

One of the first things I did was name all the hallways with school spirit phrases or something that was "JM" related. Gone were descriptors like "Math Hall," or "at the second turn." "Orange and Black Court" and the main hallway being called "James Monroe Way" became the common language. I also figured it would be easy to tell someone where a classroom was located if I could say "You are now on James Monroe Way. Stay on this hall and make a right at Tradition St., and you will see room 136 on your left." Because I wanted to reinforce aspects of architecture, geometry, tradition, and school spirit, I duplicated the names of many of the hallways on the first and second floor. I think what was cool was when I would overhear the students discussing the significance of "1951 St." or "Yellowjacket Dr." Many times, the students would go home and discuss these topics with their parents, who would usually share a story that related to that hallway/street name. Every year we wanted something new, so the building improvement after Mr. Duarte's interview, Mr. James Yager, who at the time served as mathematics department chair, mentioned to me that if I was going to hire Mr. Duarte, there might be some people who will be taken aback by this choice, and question if all students would be able to relate to the dynamics of our team. Mr. Yager was on the interview panel because I trusted him, and what he said had some credence. Mr. Yager did not see color, and treated all people the same, but he knew that there could be people in our school community that might see things differently. I spoke with Dr. Melton about this concern, and he also understood that I needed to be aware of that perception, but at the same time, if this was the person I wanted, then he would support my decision. I also spoke with some of my trusted and well-respected parents such as Charlie McDaniel to get his take on how Fredericksburg would handle having an all-black administrative team. Charlie told me that the city would be more concerned about what type of people would be hired more than the color of their skin. That was all I needed to hear. Before the day was over, I went and spoke with Mr. Duarte and offered him the job. The next week when I announced it to the faculty, they all stood and applauded Mr. Duarte on his promotion. The funny part was he had been promoted to social studies department head three weeks earlier for the new school year, and based on these circumstances, he never would get to serve in that role.

When I sat Mr. Duarte and Mrs. Rachal down in the coming weeks to discuss the upcoming school year, I had to drill home to them that based on the makeup of our admin team and the fact that everyone was watching, and in some cases waiting for us to make a mistake, we had to be perfect in every way. Mr. Duarte explained that he completely understood where I was coming from and he knew there would be certain individuals who believed he should not have gotten this position. He even told us a story about how one teacher told him before his interview that even though he was good, he couldn't become an assistant principal at the JMHS because he was black. He shook his head as he mimicked her mannerisms as she explained, "They never will have three black administrators." I wish I knew this earlier so I could have watched this teacher's reaction when I made the announcement that Mr. Duarte got the job. I bet you it would have been priceless. What a lot of people did not know was that John Duarte also had Portuguese ancestry. We had a little running joke of how we could also say he was a Hispanic hire. To add to that angle, I had Mr. Duarte start our Multicultural Action Committee, fondly known as JM MAC, to celebrate the diversity of *The* James Monroe High School. I think because many students assumed that Mr. Duarte was Hispanic, and he asked two of our female student leaders who also happened to be Hispanic to help him start the club, it started out as almost an entirely Latino organization. Then of course Mr. Duarte had to work even harder in the following years to get all students to join, and not just Hispanic students. The irony of it all.

John Duarte and Taneshia Rachal were perfect compliments to my vision of the school. Because we wanted to close the achievement gaps between all students, and we wanted to build a culture of trust amongst the faculty and students, they both were there long enough to have several allies in the building. The good part was neither of them had their own agendas, they just wanted to make the school better. The byproduct of making the school better also made their jobs easier in the long run.

I know I wanted to focus on creating more diversity in our advanced and advanced placement classes. For a school division that was approximately 45 percent African-American, you could only find one or two African-American or Hispanic-American students enrolled in upper-level courses. I spoke with many students trying to discover why this was the case, and the responses that I received were expected, but shocking. Many of the minority students informed me that they did not take upper-level courses due to not wanting to be an outlier in class. Being the only black was uncomfortable to many people, especially a sixteen or seventeen-year-old teenager. These students felt the social and sometimes even political pressure to stay in regular classes with their friends or people from their neighborhood. What made this issue even more challenging was that certain teachers would not recommend these same students, even though they had the grades and the potential to be successful in these classes. Some of the staff would argue they didn't want the student to feel all alone. One teacher even told me that she did not want to set the student up for failure. We had to change this mentality immediately!

I began to include the benefits of taking more challenging courses in my character development assemblies. I had to explain how it improves your GPA, looks good on your high school transcript, and gets you better prepared for colleges. I also had to do some selling to the parents and the African-American and Hispanic students that this was the best thing for them and it would open-up tons of opportunities in the long run. I honestly think that the students took this leap of faith because of my relationship with them. They knew that I was telling the truth and they would give it a shot. I also had to re-instruct our faculty into looking at the whole student and not just focus on their current grade in their class. Students were now going to be judged on their potential and it was our job to provide them with enough support to help them reach it. This was not an easy task, and some teachers disagreed. Those that did were strongly encouraged to teach elsewhere.

I always felt that having all our students eligible to take any class would also do great things to celebrate the diversity of our student body. We also wanted to make sure the same students were not always leading all the clubs, or being captain of the sports, teams, etc. This became a very competitive topic as many of our parents pushed their children to be involved in everything. More things to put on the high school resume so that you can get into the college of our choice. It was interesting to hear many of our students tell me that they were only applying to this college or university because their parents wanted them too. They may not have been interested in the school specifically but did so to appease their parents. This was when I had to change the tone a little in my Back to School Nights to parents to discuss some of the concerns that had been shared with me by their children. I think it came to a head for me one day when I had an honor student who also was the number one tennis player in the area rebel from his mother because she pushed him too hard. I know we hear the stories all the time about students suffering from anxiety, or external pressures that cause their grades to fall or even causing them to begin self-harming. This tennis player was a stud. He was about 6'2", had a great serve, and was a really nice kid. His mother was the typical momma bear who wanted to control every aspect of his life. She wanted me to change the entire master schedule of the school just so a specific math class would fit into his schedule. I couldn't believe it.

The stud tennis player came to apologize to me about his mom's behavior. He knew that he could attend any school of his choice, as he had several offers from great academic schools that also had solid tennis programs. He chose William and Mary early in the Spring, and by choosing early, he got to enjoy playing his senior year with no pressure. He became so fed up with how his mother was handling things that he decided to not participate in graduation. I kept wondering why he did not come to the senior picnic and why he did not show up to graduation practice. He came to see me later in the evening before graduation, just to get his graduation tickets that he promised to give to his friends. Remember on graduation day, graduation tickets are like Super Bowl tickets. If you can get your hands on some, you can almost ask for anything you want. He didn't want to celebrate his high school career but was still nice enough to make sure all his friends could have their loved ones at their graduation. A very chivalrous gesture, but sad at the same time.

By year three, we had *The* James Monroe where we wanted it. Students understood the expectation of being involved, being on time to class, and having great school spirit. The advanced courses were now diverse, and I hired enough new staff that was excited about our school atmosphere and the energy that we brought every day. As an administrator, you must make sure that you never get too comfortable in your job. I still had kids who were trying to purchase marijuana at school, and we still had a student altercation every now and then, but overall, the kids trusted that we had their backs, the faculty knew that we would provide support, and the community was pleased with the school, unless we had to discipline their child. I still needed to work on getting the right people into leadership roles for the school to move forward.

Anytime you change department heads in a building, someone is getting knocked off their peg or status in the school. My science department head was a real nice lady, pretty good teacher, but lacked overall leadership. This became very clear to me when I asked her to have a conversation with one of the members of her department because he continually would submit paperwork late. He would always get it turned in, but it still was not by the deadline. It was something that he needed to be made aware of, but not necessarily a documentable offense. She did not want to do it. She kept asking me to talk with him because that was not her thing. It was obvious that she wanted to avoid confrontation, but the teacher I asked her to speak with was not the argumentative type or a large, intimidating man. He was just a normal guy who had some tardy issues. Too many times, she declined to have conversations with staff, and it forced me to make a move. When she began to spread the word that I was opening the science department head position, it was as if she was being impeached. She had conversations with school board members, which of course got back to Dr. Melton, who inquired with me about it. When I provided him with some history, he fully supported my decision. Of course, I asked him if the expectation was for me to inform him when I made moves like that. He said, "No, unless you think it could get to a board member." This was when I had the reminder that teachers and board members run in the same circles in a small city.

I think the now former science department chair and a board member ended up having this conversation at a pool party. I swear it seems more business is conducted at the pool in Fredericksburg than anywhere else. Safe to say that I ended up getting the right person in the job that held people accountable, was good with data, and of course was very smart. We ended up making several more changes throughout our departmental leadership team in my last two years due to several people being burned out and retirements, etc. I was always big on promoting leadership in staff as well as in the students.

The entire administrative team at *The* James Monroe High School had terminal degrees. Dr. Duarte and Dr. Rachal credited me with motivating them to obtain their doctorates. First, they said I was crazy for starting a new job and a doctoral program at the same time. The school community made me feel really loved when I called Dr. Rachal to let her know that I was now Dr. Gordon, or Dr. JBG3 as I now use for marketing. The following day, when I returned to school, they had put up posters. The kids now had stickers that said to call me Dr. Gordon, and they had t-shirts made in the James Monroe colors of orange and black that had Mr. crossed through and replaced with DR. I absolutely loved it! I of course encouraged them to do the same so that they can qualify and meet the criteria of every job. I also had some conversations with Ms. Melanie Kay-Wyatt, the middle school principal, about getting her doctorate, and Taneshia spoke with Mrs. Bumbrey, one of the middle school assistant principals, about doing the same. Eventually, the entire secondary administrative teams of Fredericksburg City Public Schools had doctorate degrees. First time ever. It makes any educator feel good that they can inspire others to reach their goals while modeling that it can be done.

Year four at *The* James Monroe High School also signified the group of kids that started high school the same year that I became a principal. The previous graduating classes had at least one year with my predecessor, but this group only knew about my leadership style and the birth of *The* JM. This was the year that our scholarship money really jumped. We also were winning state titles in tennis and track, and both our girls and boys basketball teams went to the state tournament. This class trusted us. They also did a really good job of passing on our expectations to the underclassmen and told them that if they take our advice they will be fine. Word had really spread that we knew how to build relationships with students, how we knew what was going on in the school, and how we kept up with them after graduation. To me, that sounds a lot like a family. Student achievement was up, discipline was down, and the school looked the way that a premiere high school, or what I called the "Best High School in the World" should look. It became a custom at graduation that I would share personal stories that I shared with their children. Even as a principal, I bonded with these kids. I loved to cheer them on at extra-curricular activities and events, and they were amazed that I knew they did well on their chemistry test. The kids can really tell when someone cares.

Because I finished four years at a high school and did a good job of really moving the needle in student growth and achievement, job offers began to occur more frequently. Some of it had to do with my research and work with the achievement of African-American men. Dr. Marci Catlett, Deputy Superintendent of Fredericksburg City Schools, shared with Dr. Sarah Armstrong, Assistant Director for the Curry School of Education at the University of Virginia, our work in promoting more diversity in advanced classes and how the African-American men out-performed several subgroups on the English Standards of Learning assessments.

In presenting this research for the Curry School at the University of Virginia, I had several offers from school divisions to do the same for their administrative leaders and some job offers for central office positions. I never thought about what my next goal would be after becoming a high school principal. That had been my dream job for the previous four years when I first transitioned into administration. It wasn't until I got to James Monroe High School that people began to share with me how the principal of JM would many times go on to become the Superintendent of a school division and lead an organization. It was a platform for career advancement. Dr. Melton encouraged me to interview for the superintendent of Rappahannock County Public Schools so I could get some interview experience. I was hesitant because I could always remember my father saying, "Don't go after something unless you really want it." I did not want the job, as I did not see Shavonne agreeing to live there, and I was also not going to take a pay cut. This was a lesson in your work having a higher cost than the title of the position. Because I ended up being a finalist, Dr. Melton began to talk to me about my next steps and if a position was going to open in Fredericksburg. It was interesting to see how the interest from other places let my superintendent know how valuable I was.

Year five was here. When I first started as principal, I told everyone that I had a five-year plan. I am usually pretty good at meeting my goals, and knew I needed a change. That and the fact that standing on terrazzo floors for five years began to make my arches fall. Each year, I always had a new theme at *The* James Monroe High School that we would put on the back of our spirit t-shirts. Themes such as "We are The James Monroe" to "All In" to "One More." Now it was interesting that Gatorade had the same theme as we did that year, and everyone thought that was where I got it from. Pure coincidence, as "We Are The James Monroe" signified the togetherness that I mentioned previously in this chapter. Regardless of the different walks of life that we all came from, in the end, we were all Jackets. The "All In" theme rallied around giving the year everything you had. I noticed that we still had some students who were hesitant to go all in, or try new things, because they still feared failure. It could have been taking their first AP class, to trying a new sport, or joining a new club. I encouraged the students to go all in and live with the results.

The theme "One More" was a little different. I sold it as studying for one more hour, doing one more rep, or joining one more school activity. But realistically, it meant I was doing one more year. I noticed that I did not have the same amount of energy and passion as I had two years ago. I could tell because I was losing my patience on somethings that used to not bother me. I was hoping that this year was going to be like it was two years ago with the group of students that came in with me. However, this new group of students had a different viewpoint, and I wasn't sure if I could relate to them in the same way that I did with the previous cohorts. Realistically, I think I needed a change. I had an interview in one of the surrounding districts for a position that I was recruited for by those who wanted to work for me. I quickly realized there is a difference in being recruited by subordinates and being recruited by superiors. This also taught me a valuable lesson about fit.

Dr. Melton let me know that I was going to be moving into central office during a trip to Pawley's Island South Carolina to present on Ruby Payne and *Understanding Poverty*. Knowing that you are wanted always makes you feel good, but also certifies that you did a good job. It was going to be hard no longer being the principal of *The* James Monroe High School and all the SWAG that comes with it. But I knew I wanted to grow and had now set my eyes on becoming a superintendent of schools. My mother teased me that she knew that I was going to look at that as my next goal because I liked to be in charge. She was right. But I also believed that the high school principalship at *The* James Monroe High School was pretty close to being a superintendent due to the platform and politics. I just needed to learn how it worked from a central office perspective.

Chapter 7

Reflections:

Think back to your favorite principal growing up. What were some of the qualities that he/she had that made them your favorite? As a student, how did you know that the principal was doing a good job? Now compare that to your experiences with principals as an adult? Are your perceptions the same or different? If you have children, ask them how they feel about their principal or if they are out of school, how they felt about their principal? Did their principal know his/her students? Did they know their names?

Chapter 8

Leaders beyond Leaders

Many educators have always viewed central office as the "white tower" up on the hill. This is the place where many educators go at the end of their careers and forget about what it is like to be a teacher, or what it is like to be in the trenches. One of the first things Dr. Melton explained to me about being in central office meant you were there to support everyone else in the schools. It was not about you, but about how you can make those that are directly working with kids better. I knew that when I got the promotion to director of administrative services in Fredericksburg, I knew what my job responsibilities would be, but I did not fully understand that my decisions would impact more than just a school building. My decisions would have an impact on everyone, including those that did not work in schools.

As director of administrative services, I succeeded Mr. Bob Burch, who had recently retired. His title was director of operations, meaning he oversaw maintenance, construction, facilities, discipline, and any other task or duty that no one wanted to do, but also those that had to be done right. Bob was good at his job because he had so much institutional knowledge of Fredericksburg City public schools, mainly due to his forty-plus years of working in the same school division. The downside was that he was a little stuck in his ways and tended to do things a particular way because that was the way that it was always done. When I went to meet with Bob to gain a little background knowledge on my upcoming interview, I remembered him asking me "Why do you want this job? You are going to hate it." I couldn't really understand what he meant at the time, but after a little while in his position, I saw how that can could come to be true. In Bob's role, he was the guardian of the district. His, and now my, first responsibility was to protect the superintendent. This meant that we had to say no a lot. Regardless of who was asking or who someone may have owed a favor, if it was not in school board policy, or if it was something that could be considered controversial, the safe answer was to say no. The other piece of that meant you were unpopular at times because of the decisions that had to be made.

Unpopular. That word was far from my persona, as I grew up being well-liked and usually making people happy. I had to find the balance in being pleasant, but stern, and making sure that I had reasons for my decisions. Even though Bob gave me a folder that read "For John Gordon" and included templates for discipline letters, facility and maintenance contracts, and contact information for many things that would have to be done within the next few days and months, I honestly felt that he set it up like that on purpose so that I would be forced to call him. Even though Bob knew it was time to retire, he really didn't want to. He liked being in control, he liked having the ear of the superintendent, and he liked knowing we needed him. I wanted to evolve the position some to include more than just the operations side of the division. Dr. Melton and I discussed changing the title, having more buy-in into instruction, and making my responsibilities a little more prevalent to the everyday person. It was going to be a task that I was excited about, but also something I quickly found out that I had a lot to learn.

For me to fully take on this role, Dr. Melton and I talked about making the position more than operations. He knew that because of my career goals, I had to not only have a different title, but different responsibilities. We talked about making me a de facto director of secondary education since we previously discussed bringing the International Baccalaureate Program (IB) to Fredericksburg City public schools. If I wanted to continue to climb the educational career ladder, I would need to have a position that kept me close to instruction. The title of director of administrative services had a nice ring to it, and I also liked how it defined me as serving administrators. I immediately started working on bringing the IB program to Fredericksburg while I was still principal. The application process was very descriptive and tedious but was a necessity. The way IB set things up, it was a good way to find out some things about my school and my staff that I did not know. IB reviewed how many years of experience each teacher had that would instruct in the program. I also had to decide which teachers would participate and strategically deliver ways to sell the program to the school community. That was not easy as a lot of people were against it because it was new. I know I have already mentioned how people do not like change, especially if the change creates more work and asks veteran educators to change their instructional methods. For two consecutive weeks, I basically locked myself in my office to get the application done, since we were late in starting the process and the deadline was steadily approaching. When I began to have faculty meetings to explain how the IB candidate phase was a three-year process, and that I was beginning to set up school visits and training to bring the IB philosophy home, I noticed that several faculty members were not actively engaged. At first, I thought it was because they were against IB, but I was told by one of my staff confidants that it was really because they all knew I was leaving and was not going to be their principal anymore.

Being a lame-duck principal was tough. Even though I am sure that the teachers and staff still respected me, in the back of their minds because they knew I was not returning the following year, they just did not seem to be as in to it. When central office came in to have the faculty meeting with the staff to determine what characteristics and qualities they wanted in their next principal, I had to leave the meeting. Wow, being kicked out of your own faculty meeting was kind of like a jolt of reality that this thing was really happening. Dr. Melton and Bob Burch told me several times that the show must go on. That when you leave, retire, quit, or whatever, there will always be someone there to take your place. I should have known that and should have been able to accept it because I had the same feeling when I "retired" from coaching basketball. Using basketball as a metaphor, if I did a good job, and moved on to other opportunities, then one of my assistants should be able to step right in and keep the program moving forward.

It happened when I left Armstrong and Darryl Watts took over, and when I left Meadowbrook and Ksaan Brown took over. I thought the same thing could happen with the principalship. Both of my assistants, Dr. Duarte and Dr. Rachal, could do a good job in taking the school to the next level. It was just a matter of whether they wanted to, and it was also going to be a challenge for the faculty and staff to look at either of them as the principal and no longer as an assistant principal.

I began to attend more meetings outside of my building. For a while, I was really doing two jobs at once. Bob Burch had given me his priorities on what needed to be done, and even though he and I agreed on ninety percent of things, I wanted to move everything into the digital age and make everything electronic. Bob Burch wanted to physically touch every work order or request so that he could review and determine if the request was necessary. He was big on need vs. want. The only mistake that he made in doing that was because he put the wants off for so long, the back-log quickly turned everything into needs. The paper process would normally take three days. One day to be sent to Mr. Burch, one day for him to review, and one day or more to determine if the work was going to be done. By moving all work orders to being electronic, we could review requests on the same day that it was sent. This simple change took two days off the process.

Because Dr. Melton's vision was to make all of FCPS an International Baccalaureate School Division, I had a big task of getting both James Monroe High School and Walker-Grant Middle School ready for the transition to have a more student-centered instruction model. This meant that several teachers were going to have to give up their "power" of being the sole source of knowledge in the classroom. Even though research for the last ten years stated that the classroom should be more of a collaborative model with less direct instruction, many veteran teachers still taught this way because it was what they knew, and of course were the most comfortable with. I know I had two or three teachers who decided to leave James Monroe High School because they did not want to conform to "putting creativity back into instruction." Yes "putting creativity back into instruction" became the new tag line that I used to sell the program to all our school communities. Dr. Melton gave me full autonomy to make the program work and I decided to begin the diploma program at James Monroe High School first because I thought it would be easier to begin with the end in mind. Knowing what an IB graduate would look like helped to shape the Middle Year's Programme at Walker-Grant Middle School and to know what courses would need to be offered in the ninth and tenth grades at James Monroe. After Dr. Rachal was named principal and succeeded me, it made things a lot easier for the transition of getting everyone trained and along with Dr. Wyatt, the principal at Walker-Grant Middle School, we could really get the program off and running.

Meanwhile, we had to make some changes in the other departments that I was going to supervise. I was not concerned about the maintenance and facilities department at all as they were pretty much self-sufficient. The main change I implemented was creating facility coordinators (FC's) for each of our five buildings. I kind of borrowed this model from what I experienced in Chesterfield, and it worked very well. The hardest part was choosing which guys would become the FC's for each building. Now, some of the maintenance guys wanted to stay outside all day. Some of them just worked on plumbing, and others worked on HVAC. But the general maintenance employees would be the ones that would take care of work orders, that were given cellular phones, and we were off and running in the new role. The new process was so efficient, which was the overall theme of maintenance. Of course, anytime a new supervisor or boss comes onboard, there are always a few casualties of employees who just do not fit the mold of your vision, or of what needs to be done.

One of the maintenance guys seemed like he did not really want to work. He was a general maintenance contractor that had previously done some work for the superintendent. Because of this, he believed that he was special. He made up excuses on how he could not lift heavy items, or how he could not shovel snow because his doctor said he had a slight case of vertigo and that his fingers would get frost-bitten very easily. In the past, on snow days, which happened a lot in Fredericksburg, he would just drive the snow truck. These situations of course created a lot of animosity with the other members of the maintenance team as they thought that he was just trying to get over. They thought he was lazy. He also tended to miss a lot of work, which of course then created more work for the rest of the guys. He would end up being placed on restricted duty, but he used this as an excuse to do side jobs during his normal work hours, when he was supposed to be at home "sick." One of my James Monroe staff confidants saw him working on her neighbor's house across the street. She took pictures of him and sent them to me as evidence that there was nothing wrong with him. Wow. He told me and his supervisor, James Carneal, who also had great institutional knowledge of FCPS since he worked there since he was fifteen years old, that he could not climb a ladder and that he had to stay in bed all day. Meanwhile he was out cutting wood, building a deck, and painting. It was a really easy conversation to terminate his employment or suggest that "this may not be the best career" for him. James Carneal was so impressed with how I let him go, he said the termination meeting did him a favor. I guess I used the Force in that meeting.

Revising the transportation department was another story. I already heard some of the horror stories from Dr. Melton and Mr. Burch that the transportation department could not be fixed. How we always had a shortage of bus drivers, and Mr. Burch did not trust all of them. What I soon discovered was part of that synopsis was correct, but that improvements could be made. When I was introduced to the transportation department as their new boss, one of the first things I spoke about was becoming a family, and how we were going to celebrate our successes, but also that I had very high expectations. Shortly thereafter, several of the bus drivers set up meetings with me to discuss their grievances with Mr. Burch. I tried to explain that it was not about that, but they insisted on being heard. From their perspective, they felt they were not respected, they were talked down to, and there was a lot of favoritism that existed from the current transportation supervisor Mr. Washington. A lot of the things that were told to me were too raunchy and unprofessional to put into this book.

I decided to upgrade their gear. I used my Nike contract from James Monroe to buy them new shirts and sweatshirts and made sure we recognized both bus and car drivers of the month. I also increased the bonus money for perfect attendance for each month, since driver absences previously were a problem. I had some heart to heart conversations with Mr. Washington and his assistant Mr. Henderson about the perceptions the staff had about their relationship. I soon discovered the perceptions the staff had were correct, as their relationship wasn't positive. Mr. Washington felt that at times Mr. Henderson made several mistakes but was not honest about them. Mr. Henderson felt that Mr. Washington did not respect him, gave other drivers more authority than his own position, and always sided against him when it came to dealing with Mr. Burch. Well I soon discovered that they both were right. After a few months, I realized that the relationship could not be repaired, but that they were going to have to work together and remain professional to improve our transportation department. The transportation mechanic Willie, was probably the most level headed out of all three of them.

Just like any other company or job where you have many employees, there are always going to be some that rise to the top, and others that need to go. I had to terminate several drivers during my three-year tenure as director of administrative services for various reasons. All of the terminations were due to safety reasons. My first termination was due to a driver not following basic protocol. On several occasions, she would leave her bus running, with kids on the bus, and run into the school to use the bathroom, in her words, "really quick." What made matters worse was that she did not notify the school administration, transportation dispatch, or anyone that she was getting off the bus. What if one of the kids decided to get out of their seat and get behind the wheel of the bus? The first time she did this, we met, I issued her a letter of reprimand, and informed her that if she did something like that again, she would risk being terminated. Less than a month later, she did it again. I couldn't believe she argued that she had the right to get off her bus anytime that she needed to and that we were invading her privacy. Wow.

The second termination decision was made for me. One of the first drivers to come see me kept telling me stories about how she didn't think that the other drivers liked her and that some days, she did not want to come to work. Other drivers knew that she visited me several times and made a point to inform me that she was having her own issues at home and that being at work "was the safest place for her." Of course, that led me to believe that we needed to get this employee some additional assistance. About two weeks later, the local media outlet posted a story about a domestic dispute that turned deadly. As I read article, the story described a quiet home in which the mother had repeatedly been a victim of domestic violence. One day she had enough, took matters into her own hands, and shot her husband with their two children at home. Very sad. I will never forget having to travel to the local jail to deliver her termination letter with Mr. Russ. That was one of the weirdest and saddest things that I ever had to do.

The last termination I had to deal with regarded a driver that was probably too old to continue to drive. Now we all know that we cannot fire someone because of age, as that would open us up to age discrimination lawsuits. However, this senior driver was as unprofessional as they came. I am still surprised to this day that Mr. Burch did not get rid of her earlier, but maybe he was more concerned about the driver shortage. Of course, I solved that driver shortage by instituting Bus Driver Job Fairs. I was so surprised at how many people wanted to drive buses. All we had to do was get them trained, make sure they studied and knew the transportation manual (shocked that we didn't have one of those either), and then have them drive with one of our veteran drivers for a while before we turned them loose.

This senior driver was losing her eyesight. She became a danger to herself, to children, and of course to anyone else that was on the road. Before we could even discuss the fender benders that she had, like taking a turn too sharp and hitting a parked car or backing up in a cul-de-sac and hitting someone's mailbox, her issues were brought to our attention due to her demeanor with kids and parents. She yelled a lot. The sad part was that she didn't even realize she was yelling until we showed her the bus video, and of course several parent videos that were sent to us. One parent even took a picture of her pointing and fussing at her first grader. She looked so mean. To complicate matters, she would burst out in tears and cry anytime we gave her a reprimand. It was almost a defense mechanism. She made a critical mistake of telling Mr. Russ that I was out to get her because she was white. She said all I cared about were the "blacks and spics." This conversation took place in the grocery store, and she followed Mr. Russ around so much that he left without finishing his grocery list. Mr. Russ couldn't believe she was telling him these things because he is married to a Hispanic woman. Out of all the things that she did wrong, I do not think it was necessary to add "racist" to her list of issues. She was written up for the accidents and for having cigarettes on her bus. We discovered those when she smoked while we were waiting for the police to come to another fender bender. She just kept breaking protocol and she had to go. I terminated her on my last day in my role. It ended up being the right decision as she cursed at me throughout the entire meeting.

I think one of the things that I am most proud of during my days as director of administrative services is the renovation of the Original Walker-Grant School. The Original Walker-Grant School (OWG) is a historic landmark in the city of Fredericksburg. OWG was the African-American School that was used before integration. Everyone knew the school was behind the times, was not ADA compliant, and many times was ignored when it came to being properly maintained. This became a big point of discussion in the African-American community for decades, but nothing was ever done. The school had two buildings. The main building housed the Fredericksburg Regional Head Start Program and Early Childhood Special Education, which served three and four-year old students and their parents. I mention that these programs also served their parents because we set up a parent center to assist with child development techniques and potential employment training to help improve their financial wellbeing. To qualify for your child to attend the Head Start and Early Childhood Special Education programs, your total household income could not exceed $28,000. The annex building, which was located across the street, housed the Regional Alternative

Education Program-which served several local school divisions and was used for students who committed serious discipline incidents. Also located in the annex was RISE, the FCPS only alternative program-which served students who committed less serious discipline offenses, but had to be removed from the traditional school settings for a period of time; and the G.E.D. Program, which served those students who could not graduate on time, but still needed an opportunity to come out with a high school equivalency degree. The annex also housed the local Boys and Girls Club in the afternoons. Some people believed we were setting all these children up for failure because they did not have the necessary resources, specifically facilities, to be successful. It was almost as if the Head Start and Early Child Special Education students were destined to be in the alternative programs in ten to fifteen years. Or worse.

Dr. Melton hired Doug Westmoreland from Moseley Architects to conduct a facility study of all the schools in FCPS. This was a very important step as many of the central office employees were spread throughout the school division because there was not enough room for all of us to fit into the "official" central office building located on Princess Anne St. Some central office directors and their staff were located at James Monroe High School. Others were in a trailer behind Hugh Mercer Elementary School. Bob Burch, and now my new office, was in an old physical education closet in the gymnasium at Hugh Mercer Elementary School. We were all over the place. The facility study by Doug Westmoreland showed we were losing hundreds of seats for student space due to central office staff being housed in schools. The study also projected the growth of

Fredericksburg over the next ten years and how it was one of the fastest growing communities in the commonwealth of Virginia. The first step to solve the potential over-crowding issue was to put central office staff in one building. We decided that renovating OWG and placing all of us there made the most sense. Now I am not sure how well this sat with the current Regional Director of the Fredericksburg Head Start Program because I think she liked being in control of OWG. Even though she complained about how it was too hot in the summer (they only had window AC units in the classrooms and nothing for the hallways), and how the city didn't care about their program or the building.

Learning school construction was one of the best experiences that I ever had. Dr. Melton consistently told me building a school was going to look great on my resume, and it would be an experience that would help me get to where I wanted to go. He also told me I was going to be extremely busy, and that on some days, I would not have time for anything else. Well as usual he was right. The number of meetings that I had to attend as well as re-learning everything that I needed to know about school facilities from my doctoral program was a huge undertaking. The main thing about construction was making sure all plans and diagrams were accurate because as soon as the sub-contractors would come in to work, they were only going to follow what was written, even if it was obvious what was written was incorrect. My job was to make sure the construction manager I had recently hired was keen on the communication that occurred between the architects and construction company, that everything was accurate, consistent, and matched what we agreed upon when we signed the contract. Of course, I also had to add in some things to make the building stand out, since it was going to become a living museum of the spirit and culture from the Original Walker-Grant School.

I met with Mr. Buddy Herndon, President of the Walker-Grant Alumni Association, to discuss the renovation and my idea to have artifacts representing each decade on display throughout the building. He was so excited the Original Walker-Grant School was finally getting a makeover, one that was needed for almost thirty years. Buddy explained to me a lot of the history I had heard about vaguely, but not in detail. Even though Buddy was in his eighties, his mind was very sharp, and he knew the history like the back of his hand. The Walker-Grant Alumni Association was very active and partnered with the Boys and Girls Club to sponsor many summer enrichment programs to help those children that needed additional support or supervision in the summer. He made me feel so proud, but also determined to make sure that the "Walker-Grant Center" as it would now be called became a state of the art, first class facility. The renovation of the school started as a major job, but it really provided me a sense of purpose for helping a community that was ignored for so long that it had almost been forgotten.

The problem with creating such a beautiful facility meant now more people wanted to access it, or even change the rules to make it their own. The same building that was denied the funding for remodeling or renovation for decades was now being fought over like the prettiest girl in school. Local art groups were putting pressure on City Council for ownership of the new meeting room. The Walker-Grant Alumni Association was insulted by this as they felt that their wishes were being ignored by the same people who had refused funding for so long. It was my job to meet with each group and help to negotiate a compromise to make everyone happy, while still preserving the legacy of OWG. Many people in the city now looked at the school as a sign of racial tension for the control of the building. The African-American community was supporting the Walker-Grant Alumni Association because it was their school and they did many things to maintain the building over the years to the best of their ability. Parks and Recreation got involved in the "lobbying" because there were discussions about them controlling the event and rental schedule. Some of our city politicians thought this was a good idea, mainly because Parks and Recreation was under their umbrella. I think some of these same people forgot I was on the Parks and Recreation board due to my current job responsibilities. The funny part was the actual employees of the Parks Department did not want to take on that responsibility anyway. In the end, everyone came to their senses, and after some strong political lobbying by supporters of the alumni association, things remained the same as far as who could use the building and the new facilities. Dr. Melton always had planned to open the school up "more" to the community anyway.

As we were preparing to eventually move into the Walker-Grant Center, one of the last tasks that I had to do was to move all central office staff located in the school buildings into a temporary office building until the Walker-Grant Center was completed. We were provided space in the old juvenile and domestic relations court building in downtown Fredericksburg. I really believed that moving adults

was going to be easy, but I was surprised at how needy some
of them were. I ordered approximately 150 boxes per department. Mind you, because FCPS is so small, each department only consisted of a director and their administrative assistant. The problem was that so many of them were
pack rats. Bob Burch was not any different, because when I
moved, we found documents from the 1970s that no longer
had any relevance. A lot of the directors kept things that
needed to be thrown away.

As Dr. Melton, Bob Young (the director of technology),
and Dr. Melton's assistant Laura Baxter-Christopher, and
I toured the two floors we were given for our temporary
offices, the lobbying from the other departments and their
clerical staff immediately began. I came up with a simple
plan of putting sticky notes on the doors and office areas
of where each department wanted to be. Mr. Young and I
had already chosen our offices and departmental locations
in a previous visit. It was a justified perk as he and I, along
with Mike George, were responsible for setting everyone up
in their offices anyway. It was comical to watch directors
claim a space, put a sticky note on the door, and then watch
another director come by and remove it and replace it with
their own sticky note. I mean, it was almost like you could
not turn your back. Then when we set up moving dates,
using our guys from the maintenance department as the
movers, directors were trying to convince the maintenance
guys to move them later because they hadn't finished pack-
ing, or to move them earlier because they were ready to go
and were bored. I guess the schedule I sent out didn't matter, nor did the fact that some of our directors forgot that
the maintenance guys had to do their other daily work on

those days as well. Let's just say by the time we got everyone moved in, I decided to take all the maintenance guys out for a happy hour to thank them for their patience, professionalism, and mainly because they needed it for dealing with those crazy people for a week.

Things are going pretty well in year three of being Director of Administrative Services. The IB Diploma Program was up and running smoothly at James Monroe High School, and we just received the good news that both Walker-Grant Middle School and James Monroe High School were accepted into the Middle Years Program. We had zero feedback from the IB auditors on how to make sure the program was ready for implementation in the September of 2017. Lastly, both Hugh Mercer Elementary School and Lafayette Upper Elementary School had just been accepted into the candidacy phase of the IB Primary Years Program.

Of course, we now had to get everyone trained and continue to promote the positive divisional message we were using at the secondary level throughout our school communities and the city of Fredericksburg. The transportation department had new leadership and we even instituted a GPS tracking system that parents could use to track their student's buses, to and from school, as well as when they participated in extra-curricular activities. The maintenance department continued to run very smoothly, and guys enjoyed coming to work every day. The only issue we had to deal with came back to the Fredericksburg Regional Head Start program and their move from their current classrooms and office space into the newly renovated portion of the school. The entire renovation plan was to be completed

To be honest, I do not know why she acted the way she did. It delayed the entire move for almost three hours. It wasn't until I told Mr. Carneal to move "the sh*t" because I had heard enough and we were behind schedule. Mr. Carneal said I am his boss and he will do what I tell him to do as he laughed when he got off the phone. When I called Dr. Melton and explained to him what had happened, I don't think that I had ever heard him so mad in my life. He sent Deputy Superintendent Dr. Catlett over to the building to make sure that things were moving forward as we planned. Dr. Catlett worked very well in calming the situation. She also did a good job of reminding everyone involved we had to follow the plan that was agreed upon. She finally let everyone know how disappointed Dr. Melton was that things did not go smoothly, especially when dealing with adults.

Dr. Melton began to discuss his retirement. He just did not know when that was going to be. I think the belief of some people in the school division and around Fredericksburg was that I would be his successor due to my successful tenure as the principal of James Monroe High School, and with the completion of major projects and programs during my time as Director of Administrative Services. You never know what the future may hold, but I always wanted to do more. Dr. Melton taught me so much in the eight years I was with him, and it made things easier when you are working for someone who you considered a friend. I began to receive several inquiries from school divisions in the Richmond area. I always made it a point to know what was going on "back home" in case the perfect job opportunity popped open. It would have to be the perfect job for me to leave my level of autonomy, comfort, and power that I had earned in Fredericksburg. I interviewed for two assistant superintendent positions within the next year because I thought they were good fits, and in one, I was told I had the job. Dr. Melton did not want to lose me, but he knew I still wanted to grow and I had already done almost everything that I could in Fredericksburg. He also warned me you never have a job until you sign the dotted line. Being promised a job and actually having the job are two different things. It shook me to my core when the "promised" job fell through. It also let me know you cannot take everyone at their word. Dr. Melton kind of saw it coming because things were taking so long. When I spoke with Dave Sovine about the process, he also said things did not add up right. Damn. Two guys whose opinion I valued very much were saying the exact same thing. When another candidate got my "promised" position, it hurt my ego and my confidence. I began to wonder if I was as good as everyone told me I was. It wasn't until I received a call about an opening in Chesterfield County that I realized that I was still good enough to help lead a large school division.

Leading a larger school division would allow me to write my own ticket to become a superintendent. The only downside about working in a small school division is if you ever wanted to climb the ladder and become a superintendent, it would only be in another small school division. At least with a new role in a larger school division, I would now have the freedom and flexibility to get a superintendent job almost anywhere. Besides, it would be special to go back and work in the school division where my administrative career started. The hard part of course would be building new relationships with former peers, supervisors, and colleagues, as their boss. Dr. James Lane had recently been named the superintendent in Chesterfield as he was coming off being recognized as state superintendent of the year. He and I became friends from spending some time together at the national superintendent's conferences. Dr. Lane was known as being very innovative and I thought I could learn some new things from him as I continued upon my educational journey. When I was named chief academic officer in Chesterfield, the response from my former colleagues in Chesterfield was so positive. The response from my current colleagues in Fredericksburg was very sad, because they did not want to see me leave, but they understood. I was so excited at this new opportunity, but a little nervous at the same time. Shortly after I was named chief academic officer, Dr. Lane informed me that by the time July 1, 2017 came around, I would be the chief of schools. At first, I wasn't sure what that role would entail, but I liked the title of it. Dr. Lane explained that I would supervise, mentor, and coach all the principals. He told me that I had one job, which was "to get the schools popping." He said that he was so impressed with what I had done in Fredericksburg, especially during my tenure at *The* James Monroe High School (it still lives), that he wanted me to inspire our principals in Chesterfield to do the same, if not more. I was on it. It felt so good to know that the formula that I used to create an innovative and excellent educational experience was going to be the standard in Chesterfield. I was and still am so excited to be a part of the #oneccps team.

Chapter 8
Reflections:

1) What does the term leadership mean to you?

2) What do you think is the biggest challenge in becoming a leader?

3) How does a leader motivate others to follow?

4) From reading this book, have you picked up any new tips on leadership? If so, what are the tips?

Outro

It is always difficult to reflect upon your career and realize many of your experiences have shaped who you have become today, as well as helped to shape thousands of our youth. I think one of the more important things is to realize many of the life lessons, or educational experiences you had with students now are being reflected in our current school-age kids because those former students are now adults. It is always one of the best feelings in the world when one of your former students comes up to you and says you were their favorite teacher growing up, or they learned so much from you as a coach and you made them want to become one themselves. Or that they want to become an educator and eventually a principal because you made it look like fun when you did it. Powerful stuff. I am so grateful that my parents instilled in me the importance of education and how it would be the one thing that could help me reach all my goals. I am lucky that my two older sisters modeled how you could be smart and do your work to keep your parents happy, while still being cool at school to keep your status with your friends. I understand that not everyone views education in the same light I do, but I am hoping they understand the overall importance of it for their children.

I am hoping that *The Teacher's Lounge* gave all readers a historical perspective, and some insight into some of the trials and tribulations that many administrators, parents, students, and teachers go through today. It was my goal to help all of us understand that making education relative and using pop culture like sports and music will provide connections, help develop logic and insight, and will be a huge influence on how students think. As a history teacher, I would be remiss if I did not point out what happened in government and politics five and ten years ago will have a direct impact on how students and teachers are successful in school today. Funding decisions, educational platforms, and the change in how we are viewed in the world will determine which curriculums will become the focus. This is not a cycle; this is a pattern. We must understand that because we can access information instantly, we must keep education relevant, creative, and ensure we do not repeat past mistakes.

As educators, we need to ensure that we continue to provide exciting, intuitive, and practical educational experiences for our students. We must also make sure our parents, local legislators, and media outlets fully comprehend some of the challenges schools face and we provide the necessary support to help *all* our kids be successful. I know it is difficult for everyone to understand the concept of helping *all* kids. There are still some stereotypes that exist for students that we are still trying to combat. Students who are economically disadvantaged do not need their teacher treating them like they are economically disadvantaged and will always be in poverty. These students need teachers who can motivate and inspire them, but more importantly, they need teachers they can trust. All it takes is for a student to have one teacher who believed in them to make a difference in their lives. We still need more teachers and administrators that are comfortable with special education students. We need to address how some educators react to the thought of having special education students in their class. Outside of worrying about the mental limitations, or the physical handicaps, some teachers cannot handle the students because they are different. I know there are some educators out there that avoid seeing and interacting with students who have severe disabilities only because it makes them uncomfortable. However, when you take the time to get to know these kids, you will find out they are just like other kids and want the same things and have the same dreams.

I completely understand that the "hot topics" in education change every three to five years. I understand issues such as affirmative action from the early 1990s have been replaced with the need for equity in the late 2010s. I understand terminology like guidance counselors has changed to school counselors, or special education students may be called exceptional education students, but that the need to support our schools, and more importantly our kids, has not changed. Schools have become more than just a place for learning in society. Schools are now viewed as hubs of the community, as safe places for gathering, and in some cases, as a sign of hope. I didn't really understand this until I began to receive requests for individuals to have funerals at schools when I oversaw facilities for FCPS. At first it made me uncomfortable because I thought a school should just be a school. But it wasn't until I heard some of the heart felt stories from the families of those that had passed how the school meant so much to them. Or how the funeral home or church was not big enough to hold all the people who wanted to attend the funeral. The overwhelming suggestion and hope of the community was to have the funeral at the school because everyone knew where it was, and it always made people feel good when they entered. These are the life lessons that you can only gain through experience, and the proof that a school is more than a school.

What are you going to do to make things better? As an educator, or just an avid reader, how will you take the information shared in this text and apply it to the real world? Anytime there is new information out there, or something that needs to be shared, the first, and many times the most important aspect is awareness. At the conclusion of this book, you now understand what it is like to be an educator today. Besides what you see on the news, you now understand all school communities face similar challenges, but those challenges can be overcome solely based on the relationships between administrators, parents, students, and teachers. If the positive relationships extend to bus drivers, custodians, maintenance staff, and support staff, we tremendously increase the overall success rate for the student. In the end, it's about the kids. Right?

I would like to personally thank all the students, teachers, basketball players, coaches, parents, and administrators that I worked with since I began my career in education in 1995. From a substitute teacher on the Eastern Shore of Maryland to my current role as chief of schools for

Chesterfield County Public Schools, I could not have accomplished and learned so much without all of you. Thank you for your support, the tough lessons, and the trust you instilled in me to help your kids learn and grow. Thank you to the adults who let me be myself and helped to foster the leadership ability I had inside. I hope everyone who reads this book will be able to take something away from it that makes them a better educator, but more importantly, a better person. If we are doing our jobs as educators correctly, we will produce more people who believe in education as much as we do.

About the Author

Dr. John B. Gordon III was born in Richmond, Virginia. He is the youngest of three children to Mr. John B. Gordon, Jr. and Marian J. Bey Gordon. He learned so many great things from his two older sisters, Rhea and Donna, specifically getting numerous insights into what the future of his educational career would look like because they were five and six years older. Dr. Gordon attended Henrico County Public Schools, matriculating through Maude Trevett Elementary School, Brookland Middle School, and Hermitage High School.

John really enjoyed his years at Hermitage High School where he was a standout basketball player and developed a strong passion for psychology. Dr. Gordon earned his bachelor of arts in pyschology from the University of Virginia in 1995 and later returned to earn his master of education with a concentration in history in 2000. He also earned a post-master's certificate in administration and supervision from Virginia Commonwealth University in 2007 and completed his doctoral studies at Virginia Tech in 2012.

He began his teaching career as a substitute teacher on the eastern shore of Maryland, and later taught fifth grade at East Salisbury Elementary School. John returned to Richmond and taught history at his parents' alma mater, Armstrong High School, from 1997-2002. Coach Gordon also served as the head boys' basketball coach from 1998-2002 winning the Capital District title and coach of the year honors after the 2001-2002 season. Coach Gordon then moved to Meadowbrook High School in Chesterfield County where he served as a head basketball coach, history teacher, and assistant athletic director. At Meadowbrook High School, Coach Gordon built a championship program and a level of team chemistry and camaraderie that is still strong to this day. At Meadowbrook, the men's basketball teams won back-to-back Central District titles, numerous tournament championships, and the Central Region of Virginia championship. His teams made the second state appearance in school history, and he earned Central District coach of the year and currently has the highest winning percentage in school history. John crossed the bridge into administration beginning in the 2005-2006 school year when he served as dean of students and later as an assistant principal at Meadowbrook High School.

Retiring from coaching after the 2007–2008 season, Dr. Gordon transferred to Monacan High School in Chesterfield, Virginia where he served as an assistant principal for one year. Beginning in the 2009–2010 school year, Dr. Gordon was named the principal of James Monroe High School in Fredericksburg, Virginia. He served in that role for five years where he successfully increased the graduation rate, reduced the dropout rate, started the International Baccalaureate Program, increased minority student achievement and participation in advanced courses, and led the school to being ranked in the top seven percent of high schools by *U.S. News and World Report*. Dr. Gordon was promoted to director of administrative services for Fredericksburg City Public Schools beginning in the 2014–2015 school year. In this role, Dr. Gordon led the initiative for the implementation of the International Baccalaureate Program at all schools in the division, the renovation of the original Walker-Grant School, and the development of administrative coaching programs. Dr. Gordon was named the chief of schools for Chesterfield County Public Schools for the 2017–2018 school year. He currently works with sixty-four principals in the fifth largest school division in Virginia. He works to develop a leadership framework that is focused on principal talent management that includes principal mentoring and coaching models, instructional leadership, and a service mindset for all students.

Dr. Gordon is also president of Schools That Inspire, LLC, where he has applied all of the principles of building positive and supporting school communities; delivering inspirational messages to the faculty, staff, and students; and providing edutainment to keep everyone excited about the field of education.

Dr. Gordon is married to his wife Shavonne, and they have three children: Marcus, Kennedy, and Simone.

SCHOOL *Maude Trevvett* YEAR *82*
CITY *Henrico* STATE *Va*
AGE *8* HEIGHT *4'7* WEIGHT *74*

3RD GRADE

FILE NEWSPAPER CLIPPINGS,
REPORT CARDS, CLASS LISTS,
PHOTOS AND OTHER SCHOOL
MEMENTOS INSIDE THIS ENVELOPE.

John Gordon III
MY SIGNATURE

3rd grade is an important time in elementary school. I was a little nervous to smile and show my teeth because my friends and I would tease each other on who had the "buck teeth." But worse than that, why did my mom decide to put me in that turtleneck?

In school, if you earned the Presidential Physical Fitness Award, it meant you were one of the best athletes in your grade. I think I earned this award every year until they introduced the mile run in 10th grade. I still can't run long distance!

I really believe that all of those years of riding my ten-speed paid off. Air Gordon was real! I had drawings and posters circulating around school. This pic shows some of the "ups" and what many don't know is that I came from the other-side and did a 360 under the rim!

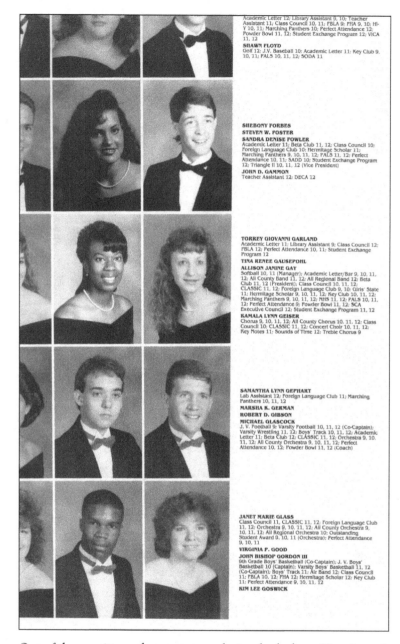

Academic Letter 12; Library Assistant 9, 10; Teacher Assistant 11; Class Council 10, 11; FBLA 9; FHA 9, 10; Hi-Y 10, 11; Marching Panthers 10; Perfect Attendance 12; Powder Bowl 11, 12; Student Exchange Program 12; VICA 11, 12

SHAWN FLOYD
Golf 12; J.V. Baseball 10; Academic Letter 11; Key Club 9, 10, 11; PALS 10, 11; SODA 11

SHEBONY FORBES
STEVEN W. FOSTER
SANDRA DENISE FOWLER
Academic Letter 11; Beta Club 11, 12; Class Council 10; Foreign Language Club 10; Hermitage Scholar 11; Marching Panthers 9, 10, 11, 12; PALS 11, 12; Perfect Attendance 10, 11; SADD 10; Student Exchange Program 12; Triangle II 10, 11, 12 (Vice President)

JOHN D. GAMMON
Teacher Assistant 12; DECA 12

TORREY GIOVANNI GARLAND
Academic Letter 11; Library Assistant 9; Class Council 12; FBLA 12; Perfect Attendance 10, 11; Student Exchange Program 12

TINA RENEE GAUSEPOHL
ALLISON JANINE GAY
Softball 10, 11 (Manager); Academic Letter/Bar 9, 10, 11, 12; All County Band 11, 12; All Regional Band 12; Beta Club 11, 12 (President); Class Council 10, 11, 12; CLASSIC 11, 12; Foreign Language Club 9, 10; Girls' State 11; Hermitage Scholar 9, 10, 11, 12; Key Club 10, 11, 12; Marching Panthers 9, 10, 11, 12; NHS 11, 12; PALS 10, 11, 12; Perfect Attendance 9; Powder Bowl 11, 12; SCA Executive Council 12; Student Exchange Program 11, 12

KAMALA LYNN GEISER
Chorus 9, 10, 11, 12; All County Chorus 10, 11, 12; Class Council 10; CLASSIC 11, 12; Concert Choir 10, 11, 12; Key Notes 11; Sounds of Time 12; Treble Chorus 9

SAMANTHA LYNN GEPHART
Lab Assistant 12; Foreign Language Club 11; Marching Panthers 10, 11, 12

MARSHA K. GERMAN
ROBERT D. GIBSON
MICHAEL GLASCOCK
J. V. Football 9; Varsity Football 10, 11, 12 (Co-Captain); Varsity Wrestling 11, 12; Boys' Track 10, 11, 12; Academic Letter 11; Beta Club 12; CLASSIC 11, 12; Orchestra 9, 10, 11, 12; All County Orchestra 9, 10, 11, 12; Perfect Attendance 10, 12; Powder Bowl 11, 12 (Coach)

JANET MARIE GLASS
Class Council 11, CLASSIC 11, 12; Foreign Language Club 11, 12; Orchestra 9, 10, 11, 12; All County Orchestra 9, 10, 11, 12; All Regional Orchestra 10; Outstanding Student Award 9, 10, 11 (Orchestra); Perfect Attendance 9, 10, 11

VIRGINIA F. GOOD
JOHN BISHOP GORDON III
9th Grade Boys' Basketball (Co-Captain); J. V. Boys' Basketball 10 (Captain); Varsity Boys' Basketball 11, 12 (Co-Captain); Boys' Track 11; Air Band 12; Class Council 11; FBLA 10, 12; FHA 12; Hermitage Scholar 12; Key Club 11; Perfect Attendance 9, 10, 11, 12

KIM LEE GOSWICK

One of the unwritten rules was to try to be involved a lot at Hermitage. It became a little bit of a competition to see who could have the most activities while in school. Not bad for a guy who was told that he did not take school seriously in kindergarten.

Personality: John B. Gordon III

Spotlight on chairman of the Virginia High School League

John B. Gordon III has fond memories of playing basketball for Hermitage High School in Henrico.

"I loved my high school career," the 40-year-old Richmond native says, calling it a big influence on his decision to become a teacher and later coach boys basketball at two area high schools, Armstrong and Meadowbrook.

Dr. Gordon, who has an Ed.D. from Virginia Tech, now is happy to hold an important role in ensuring sports continues to be a big part of the lives of today's high school students.

Principal at a Fredericksburg high school, Dr. Gordon is the new chairman of the executive committee of the Virginia High School League, the governing body for state high school sports.

Ken Tilley, VHSL executive director, lauded Dr. Gordon's election, saying the new chairman "he has clearly distinguished himself as an outstanding leader — and we look forward to a successful and progressive year as he presides" over the VHSL.

Dr. Gordon is the first African-American to head the 100-year-old VHSL, which oversees 71 state championships in 27 sports in which 180,000 students participate each year.

He was elected for a one-year term to the top VHSL volunteer post in his third year on the 28-member committee. He served as chairman-elect last year and earlier as chairman of Region I, which includes Fredericksburg.

He is convinced that students who play sports are in a better position "to reach their

potential.

It gives them a sense of belonging to something positive and greater opportunities for success."

He is taking on the chairmanship at a time of change for VHSL schools. This year, he and the other committee members are involved in making sure the VHSL revamped the way the state's 316 high schools are classified is successful.

The revamp wiped out the former A, AA and AAA classifications and the former regions.

Effective this year, VHSL has placed each school in one six new classifications based on enrollment in a bid to improve competition. The new classifications range from 1A for schools with 450 or fewer students to 6A for schools with 1,860 or more students.

For example, the five Richmond high schools in the VHSL

— Armstrong, George Wythe, Huguenot, John Marshall and Thomas Jefferson — now are classified as 3A. They play in a new 3A East conference that includes Petersburg and Hopewell high schools.

"I look forward to being the chairman as the new six classification process gets under way this school year," he says.

A close-up of this week's Personality John B. Gordon III, who is combining his dual interests in education and sports:

Occupation: Principal of The James Monroe High School in Fredericksburg. I am the first African-American principal in the history of James Monroe.

Current home: Glen Allen.

Alma maters: University of Virginia, bachelor's degree in 1995 and master's degree in 2000; Virginia Tech, doctoral degree, 2012.

Family: Married my college sweetheart Shavonne Banks Gordon, on May 31, 1997; son, Marcus, 22, a senior at Longwood University; daughters, Kennedy, 9, a fourth-grader in the gifted and talented program at Echo Lake Elementary; and Simone, prekindergarten pupil at the Primrose School.

Reaction to being VHSL's first African-American chairman: I had no idea that I was the first African-American chairman of the league until Bruce Bowen, former athletic director at Hermitage High School, and current chairman of the VIAAA

informed me one day at the executive committee meeting. It is my job to make sure that I am not the last African-American or minority chair.

Highest position previously held by a person of color: We have had several minorities on the executive committee and a few have been chairman-elect, but for a variety of reasons they never ascended to the position of chair.

VHSL's No. 1 objective and its status: The top objective of the League is to encourage student participation in desirable school activities by conducting or supporting programs of interscholastic activities in all fields.

How VHSL programs are financed: Programs are financed by the annual membership fee that all schools must pay.

Why sports is important: Because it keeps students motivated to come to school, reduces the dropout rate and provides opportunities for leadership and growth. I loved my high school career, which is part of the reason why I became a teacher and a coach. I honestly feel that involvement in school helps students to reach their potential and gives them a sense of belonging to something positive.

Sports hero and reason: they are my hero: As a kid, my favorite basketball players were Ron Harper and Michael Jordan. Currently, I think LeBron James is the most athletic basketball player I have ever seen.

Leadership is: It can be inherited, it can be developed, but it must be sustained. Leaders must have a plan. Leaders must lead

Please turn to B2

Thank you to the *Richmond Free Press* for covering this accomplishment. I did not know that I was the first African-American Chair in the 100-year history of the Virginia High School League until my Hermitage A.D. Bruce Bowen told me at a meeting. Talk about lifelong relationships...

Endorsements

"Dr. Gordon is an intelligent, motivated, and highly driven educator. His passion and focus on putting students' needs first in all decision making processes is an admirable trait that highly impactful leaders strive to emulate. John's energy, innovative approach, and advocacy for leveling the playing field for underrepresented student groups have been game changers for the many students he has touched and inspired throughout his educational journey."

Dr. David Sovine
Superintendent of Schools
Frederick County Public Schools

"The stories, theories, and practices outlined in Dr. John Gordon's book The Teacher's Lounge are inspiring reminders about the power of a loving approach to engaging, educating, and empowering learners."

Dr. Luvelle Brown
Superintendent of Schools
Ithaca City School District

"What can you say about someone who you worked very closely with for eight years, who became a close friend and who you had the pleasure of watching grow personally and professionally? I saw John evolve into a well-respected administrator, a man who valued all people, who lead through collaboration and example. This book brought back some very fond memories."

Dr. David G. Melton
Superintendent of Schools
Fredericksburg City Public Schools

"John B. Gordon III has written a book that will benefit many who work with children. He brings an interesting perspective of comparing his reality of growing up in a Virginia suburb with youngsters growing up in urban environments. He contends that although the two "worlds" are different, there is much that is similar. I will consider The Teacher's Lounge to be a must read for educators at all levels."

Principal Kafele
Principal Kafele Consulting, LLC
PrincipalKafele.com

Printed in the USA
CPSIA information can be obtained
at www.ICGtesting.com
JSHW052304280723
45617JS00001B/1

9 781948 484466